WHAT READERS ARE SAYING ABOUT

The Precipice of Life: Leadership and Personal Growth Insights from a Mountaineer's Edge

"Bo is living proof that we can learn the most valuable and profound life lessons when we leave safe zones behind and venture into the wilderness, closing in on the precipice of life to find ourselves."

—**Marcus Bauer,** Founder of Goalscape Software

"The journey of mountain climbing is the perfect metaphor for the journey of life. This is the starting point for Bo Parfet's powerful new book, *The Precipice of Life.* It's a book that brings Parfet's learnings from scaling the world's tallest peaks to the everyday life challenges of leadership, achieving success, and living a full life in the modern age that we all face."

—**Nate Klemp, PhD,** Coauthor of *The 80/80 Marriage and The New York Times* Bestseller *Start Here: Master the Lifelong Habit of Wellbeing.*

"I love it!! It is powerful, authentic, persuasive, compelling, inspiring, and filled with wisdom! The climbing metaphor is spot on in everything we do in life. This is a must-read for everyone."

—**Jim Loehr, EdD**, World-renowned Performance Psychologist, Bestselling Author and Co-Founder of the Johnson and Johnson Human Performance Institute

"Journey within. It's the clarion call of this provocative book that challenges the reader to take on their innermost obstacles in pursuit of alignment with one's authentic self. Powerful, compelling, and literally breathtaking, it's a must-read for those on the most important journey of their lives."

—**Simon Mainwaring,** Founder/CEO of
We First and *Wall Street Journal* Bestselling
Author of *Lead With We*

"The Precipice of Life is for anyone looking to explore the inner depths of their soul's calling. The stories from others who have contributed and the advice from the authors are engaging, thought-provoking, and worth contemplation if you want to live a life that is heartfelt and driven by your dreams."

—**Cynthia Covey Haller,** Author of *Live Life in Crescendo*

"It's hard to overstate the need for conscious leadership in today's world. Simple and inspiring, Bo demonstrates how true leaders face challenges, access inner wisdom, practice humility, and continually transform in all aspects of life."

—**Maryanne O'Brien,** Author of *The Elevated Communicator:
How to Master Your Style and Strengthen Well-Being at Work*

"Life is an expedition, literally! In this wonderfully engaging book, you will learn expedition life lessons on letting go, that falling is not failure, and that curiosity is a driving force for happiness and a meaningful life from a master teacher. Don't miss it!"

—**Chester Elton,** known as the Apostle of Appreciation,
and Bestselling Author of *Leading with Gratitude*

"Being an adventurer and someone who appreciates the risks associated with exploration, Bo Parfet's new book, "The Precipice of Life," will give the readers insights into living a life that is so rich with experience and the ability to achieve more than you ever expected. He shares his stories and adventures and those of many other climbers and athletes that have risked doing what they love and are passionate about doing. It is a must-read for anyone who is looking to engage and appreciate the richness of life, people, and events that guide their destiny."

— **Gregg Treinish,** Executive Director of Adventure Scientists®

"If one is looking for a healthy dose of insight and perspective from an author who has experienced going to the ends of the earth and back, then one will want to read *The Precipice of Life* by Bo Parfet. His experience as an entrepreneur and mountaineer, accented with his human life stories, will move you to take action and change your life for the better."

— **Robie Vaughn,** Entrepreneur, Author, Speaker, Olympic Athlete, Everest Summiteer

"Excellent insight. Profound enthusiasm. Experiential expertise. Bo possesses all of this and more as he takes us on an adventure that literally takes us to the edge. He beckons us to dig a little deeper into our souls and to be comfortable with being uncomfortable. Once you start reading, you won't put it down until you are done, and you will be asking for more."

— **Jason Valadao,** US Naval Officer, Author of *Exceptional Every Day,* and Team physician for the United States Naval Academy

"Whether you are an entrepreneur, an exhausted parent, a young person trying to figure out their 'why,' a professional who feels like no matter how hard they work, it's just **not** working, the metaphor of climbing a mountain is real. There are many stages in life when it feels like you have to start all over again, and you are standing at the base of the mountain, looking up. And the overwhelming feeling is, 'Will I make it?'. What this book does is take you by the hand and show you that step by step, you *can* make it, even when every step is a struggle. Thank you, Bo, for helping all of us on our journey!"

—**Elizabeth Gould,** Reinvention Coach, Speaker, and Bestselling Author of *Feeling Forwards: How to Become the Person Who Has the Life You Want*

"I personally know the power of action in one's life, as well as building deep relationships with a win-win mentality. In Bo Parfet's intriguing new book, *The Precipice of Life: Leadership and Personal Growth Insights from a Mountaineer's Edge*, you will be on the edge of your seat reading the harrowing stories about climbing the seven summits of the world while learning what it takes to accept our failures and push on in life. You will also understand that the Sherpas in your life are the most important guides on any journey you face. I highly recommend reading this book and would encourage you to explore your personal precipice of your life. It will help you turn any obstacles into an opportunity."

—**Dr. Greg Reid,** Award-winning Author, Keynote Speaker, Film Producer of *Three Feet From Gold-Turn Your Obstacles into Opportunities*

"To reach the greatest heights possible, we must be willing to confront our biggest fears. The lessons that Bo Parfet shares in *The Precipice of Life* will help you to pursue your true potential and overcome any obstacle that stands in your way."

— **David Meltzer,** Co-founder of Sports 1 Marketing,
Bestselling Author and Top Business Coach

"The precipice of life is a magical place; it transforms the willing soul who — looking beyond the safety of the known — realizes that what it has been created to be — awaits it *just over the edge*. This is the 'fear-busting' message that Bo Parfet shares with his readers, even as he invites them to discover its liberating truth for themselves."

— **Guy Finley,** Bestselling Author of *Letting Go*

As a CEO, neurosurgeon, and advocate for optimal health, I know the importance of dedication and focus required to achieve optimal results. Bo Parfet in his new book, *The Precipice of Life*, provides the readers with insights and guidance on how to focus to achieve optimal human performance, whether training to climb Everest or achieving any difficult goal. Bo shares the formula of inspiration and grit to achieve optimal results. This is a must-read for anyone wanting to move beyond the ordinary.

— **Robert Hariri M.D., Ph.D.,** Founder, Chairman, and CEO of
Celularity, Co-founder, Fountain Life and Human Longevity
Bestselling Author of *LifeForce*

"Life is about being organized and prepared. It is about getting things done and enjoying what you are doing while following your purpose and mission.

"In *The Precipice of Life,* author Bo Parfet shares the lessons he has learned as a mountaineer, having climbed the seven highest summits in the world—and as an entrepreneur and leader. His insights and the lessons of over twenty other extreme athletes and thought leaders interviewed for the book will provide you with the inspiration, spark, and drive to propel you to achieve the most important plans in your life. This is a must-read for anyone wanting to reach a greater level of human potential and enjoy the journey along the way."

—**Scott Duffy,** Speaker, Entrepreneur, Business Strategist, and
Author of *Breakthrough-How to Harness the Aha!*
Moments That Spark Success

"*The Precipice of Life* is one of those books that inspires you to go out and conquer your fears, to move beyond the obstacles that might be holding you back, but most importantly, to mold you as the leader that you need to become to climb a mountain or guide your organization to success. This book is loaded with practical advice from Bo Parfet, the author, and from the over twenty adventurers and thought leaders who have shared their insights and wisdom about leadership, failures, and enduring tough times to succeed at anything you put your mind to."

—**Scott Jeffrey Miller,** Multi-Bestselling Author of the
Master Mentors Series, Radio & Podcast Host,
and Global Keynote Speaker

"*The Precipice of Life* is a must-read for anyone hoping to access the incredible level of commitment, curiosity, leadership, and humility required to step into the unknown and take on new challenges and reach higher summits. Filled with inspiring stories, insights, and practical tools, you will learn how to cultivate the awareness, skills, and inner resources in support of living a full life.

> —**Amy Jen Su,** Executive Coach and Author of *The Leader You Want to Be: Five Essential Principles for Bringing Out Your Best Self*

"If our ultimate goal is to become the best versions of ourselves, is that more likely to happen in our comfort zone or in adversity? The author of *The Precipice of Life* subscribes to the belief that our ultimate challenges are actually our ultimate blessings. Forthright, powerful, and pulling no punches, the book suggests the perfect mindset for our hard times."

> —**Dr. Rick Stevenson,** Filmmaker, Author of *21 Things You Forgot About Being a Kid* Family Man, Baggage Handler

"Bo is clearly not controlled by fear. Because of this, he's ventured into areas of life to which few go... and come back with life lessons for all."

> —**Mark Pecota,** CEO & Co-Founder LaunchBoom.com

"How do we bring a sense of wonder and wisdom into our day-to-day lives and leadership? *The Precipice of Life* offers practical strategies to help us live and lead more consciously, effectively, and well."

> —**Renee Moorefield,** PhD, CEO, Wisdom Works Group

"Bo Parfet is no stranger to taking risks and living life to the fullest. In his book *The Precipice of Life* he weaves in his personal story and the stories of many other leaders and extreme athletes that have ventured into a similar path paved with dedication, grit, and the willingness to explore and be curious. This book will allow the reader to look deep at their own life, and contemplate how they want to create a vision for their future life, it is compelling and exciting and the lessons learned are innumerable."

— **Peter Fioretti,** Founder and CEO Mountain Funding
First Unassisted Trecker to reach the North Pole in 2018

"Whether you're scaling a mountain or growing a business, there are many similarities. Each arena demands we show up at our best, be cognizant of our surroundings, and have astute awareness and respect for the people with whom we navigate through our days.

Bo Parfet has captured this in his new book, *The Precipice of Life*. It provides the readers with insight, wisdom, and practical advice on how to tackle near any obstacle."

— **Robert Taubman,** CEO, Taubman Properties

"If you are looking for a book that will inspire you to think differently and pour more meaning into your life. You found it!"

— **Lloyd Reeb,** Real Estate Developer, Author, TED
Speaker, and Founding Partner of Halftime Institute

"Bo is a living example of someone who Lives Fully—who pursues personal growth and multiple obsessions simultaneously. Bo is making an impact on the world as well as everyone he comes in contact with. This book is for anyone who wants more out of life and knows they are capable of making a massive impact in the world, in their community, and in their family."

— **Don Wenner,** Founder and CEO of DLP Capital

THE

LEADERSHIP AND PERSONAL GROWTH

PRECIPICE

INSIGHTS FROM A MOUNTAINEER'S EDGE

OF LIFE

BO PARFET

WITH KATHY SPARROW AND GREG VOISEN

Denali Venture Philanthropy, LLC
Boulder, CO

The Precipice of Life: Leadership and Personal Growth Insights from a Mountaineer's Edge by Bo Parfet Copyright © 2023

Denali Venture Philanthropy, LLC
Boulder, CO
Website: www.theprecipiceoflife.com

First Edition: February 2023

Design by Teagarden Designs
Cover design by Michael Windsor
Front Cover Image © David Trood / DigitalVision / Getty Images

Library of Congress Control Number: 2022924154

979-8-9874372-0-9 — Paperback
979-8-9874372-1-6 — Hardcover
979-8-9874372-2-3 — eBook

AUTHOR'S NOTE

I believe positivity is contagious. I also believe negativity is contagious. *The Precipice of Life: Leadership and Personal Growth Insights from a Mountaineer's Edge* was created to be a positive influence on people's lives and to help them grow. This book aims to make an impact on the world and generate a ripple effect of positivity. Of course, this book is not for everyone. If you are not on a personal growth journey and have no desire to adopt a growth mindset, no problem, no big deal, this book isn't for you. And that's ok. Pass it along to someone who might be on that path.

Bo Parfet

CONTENTS

FOREWORD

The wind-scoured, sub-zero, harsh landscape of the Tibetan plateau is an unforgiving environment at the best of times, let alone in late Autumn time. Thus far, we've spent three days bouncing in the back of land cruisers as we make our way to Cho Oyu, the world's sixth-highest mountain. Everyone is tired, dirty, hungry, and bored.

One character is constantly bouncing between the cars, with a mop of hair and a larger-than-life, even brash, American persona combined with a big, boyish grin. He's making sure people have water, cracking (rubbish) jokes, high-fiving and fist-pumping the drivers, and doing everything we all should be doing to keep morale high, yet none of us are. His confidence is as contagious as it is bulletproof. This is my first real memory of Bo.

A few weeks later, several people are getting ready to leave the expedition, ground down by the altitude and hardships that the mountain has presented us. Our last night all together in the mess tent has an almost biblical feel to it, heads are bowed, and no one is making eye contact: truly the last supper. Then toward the end of the meal, Bo jumps up. He doesn't really ask, more he tells us that he'd like to say a few words. Standing at the end of the table, he recounts the impact our friends have had on him (us) over the last few weeks, the experiences we have shared; he bids them fair onward travels and then launches into a monologue taken from a speech from Abraham Lincoln. Some of the Brits in the tent, unused to such forthright, uninhibited prose, sniggered into their meal, but I found myself admiring it. Not only was it heartfelt (and true), but it lifted the gloom; the evening became a celebration.

Bo's superpower is his ability to always pull the positive out of a situation, be it on a mountain, in a board room, or "simply" being

Dad. It's incredible; some would say infectious. How you translate this into written text is something of a mystery, a mystery that Bo has gone some way to unlock.

Flipping through the pages of this, Bo's second book, I'm struck by the home truths he writes about, the personal learning he is willing to share, and above all, the vulnerability that he is willing to show.

I remember once, on Manaslu (the world's eighth-highest mountain), Bo came up to me asking for advice. The team he had joined wasn't working well together; the leaders were too caught up with personal ambition, leaving Bo to try and make decisions beyond what he was capable of or expected to make, yet he took the task on. Wandering into our camp, he used the no-nonsense approach he always does, getting straight to the point, not being too proud to ask, and listening intently as I explained how I'd try to extract myself from the situation he found himself in…. he possibly even made notes, that's the Bo way. Manaslu ultimately didn't work out for Bo, but he saw it as simply another necessary hurdle in the journey that he was (and still is on) rather than failure.

It's not simply the mountains; it's business and, indeed, life itself that Bo excels in. Of course, there are the wins and the losses, the elation and the grief, from death on the mountain to a catastrophic collapse of a business. But this is the very reason why Bo can sit and write this book. It's said that one must tread the fine line between success and failure to live life. Bo has had more than a foot on both sides of that line numerous times.

My wife and I have a saying in our house here in the English countryside whenever we are faced with a different decision that has far-reaching consequences. We look at each other and say out loud, "What would Bo do?" I think that says it all.

Kenton Cool
October 2022

Have You Ever Listened?
by
Jason D. Bland

Have you ever taken a moment
to listen to the air
to close your eyes
look to the sky
and listen for the breeze?

Have you ever taken a moment
to listen to the birds
to close your eyes
face the sun
feel its warmth
and listen for new songs and melodies?

Have you ever taken a moment
to listen to the earth
to stop and crouch
to draw close
and listen for life as it moves and grows?

How sweet it is
to stop
to listen
to hear
with heart and soul
all that is here, present, given
a gift—
if only we will receive it.

Jason D. Bland is the author of *Life in Four Seasons: A Collection of Poems on Nature, Wonder, and Transformation.* "Have You Ever Listened" is reprinted here with permission.

"Respond to every call that excites your spirit."

— Rumi

THE MOUNTAINS ARE CALLING

I was twelve years old when I saw the mountains for the first time, in particular the mountains at Big Sky, Montana. I peered through the window of the car as my father drove us into town. My mind whirled, attempting to capture the breathtaking beauty surrounding me from nearly every direction. Engulfed in the majesty of those peaks, their embrace soothed my soul, awakening me to a desire so strong that I knew my life would never be the same. We didn't have any mountains like that in Michigan, where I spent my childhood. The vista absolutely took my breath away.

That week I was mesmerized by those snow-capped peaks. I didn't believe that something so beautiful could be on this earth. The whole time we were there, I skied from sunup to sundown. I didn't even want to go inside to eat. I longed to become one with those mountains,

During that trip, I asked my dad, "How do I live here?"

That's a pretty big thing to think about when you're twelve, right? Yet, I felt so drawn to those mountains. I was ready to leave Michigan and my family. The calling was magnetic.

My family and I did one more trip during my teen years. The effect was the same. I had to be near the mountains. I knew that if I lived elsewhere, I'd miss out.

When I shared my thoughts with my dad, he said, "You could always go to college in Colorado." So that's just what I did.

Barely nineteen when I landed in Colorado, the intoxication of the mountains was as exhilarating as it had ever been. Within the first twenty-four hours of arriving in Fort Collins, I climbed two mountains. As I was studying (or trying to), I would glance out the windows of my dorm room at the peaks, and the longing to be on a trail overtook me—and then I'd climb, setting my studies aside for something that had latched onto me like nothing else I had ever experienced. Unlike most kids who would party as undergrads, I was getting drunk on those peaks. At the same time, they were also my cathedral. Unfortunately, the results were pretty much the same—Ds and Fs trailed across my transcript.

I had lost all sense of space and time at the foot of the Rockies—and listened even more intently to a call that took me away from family, books, and life as I had known it—or a life that was expected of me.

My Quest Began

And so began a lifelong quest to explore the mountains and ultimately climb the Seven Summits, which I described in my first book, *Die Trying.* Yet, the reason I climbed then is somewhat different than I do now. In my twenties and my early thirties, my main goal was to summit and then do it again on a different mountain. I was checking boxes off a bucket list. That said, I was also beginning to explore my inner world too. I didn't realize it at the time, but I was running from something — from myself, from a pain so deep inside of me that I was unwilling to look at it. In retrospect, I didn't feel like I was good enough. My self-worth and self-esteem were low. I struggled with dyslexia, ADHD, and a speech impediment throughout much of my earlier life. Everything was hard for me in elementary, junior, and high school. I didn't expect it to be any different in college or even in my early career.

The mountains became a way I transformed those stumbling blocks into stepping-stones. Each time I descended from a summit, I felt reborn. I had an opportunity for a new beginning. I knew if I could endure the pain and suffering of climbing, especially in some of the most challenging and dangerous conditions, then I knew I could face anything — if I wanted to.

A Call Heard by Many

Other than that initial trip with my father to the mountains in Montana, my interest in the adventures that lie outside my life in Michigan was also sparked by magazines. Many extreme sports athletes echo similar sentiments. Some were drawn to their adventures later in life, but their yearning was often ignited by other people's adventures witnessed in magazines, newscasts, and movies in their earlier years.

Robie Vaughn, an entrepreneur and longtime member of the Explorer's Club, who helped reignite the sport of Skeleton in the Olympics, says his interest in climbing, skiing, and exploring the outdoors, as well as space exploration, began with subscriptions to *Popular Mechanics* and *National Geographic*. His parents also blessed him with many travel experiences when he was young.

From the time she was a young girl, Alison Levine, who led the first American Women's Everest Expedition, was very intrigued by the stories of the early Arctic and Antarctic explorers. "Eventually, this light bulb just went on in my head. I wanted to know what it was like going to these remote environments, instead of just reading or watching documentary films about them," she shares. "I had to ask myself: Why can't I do it, too?"

Yes, she could, and she did, many times over. Alison has also climbed the highest peak on each continent and skied to both the North and South Poles—a feat known as the Adventure Grand Slam, which only twenty people in the world have achieved.

Yet, our mountains don't always have to be built out of cragged rocks or snow-packed peaks. My colleague, Claudia Schiepers, Managing Principal at DLP, was influenced by a family with a very strong work ethic. Her drive charted her course from working in the communications and marketing department for Thompson Multimedia to decades of experience in several corporations.

Like my experience glimpsing the mountains for the very first time in Big Sky, Claudia had a pivotal moment in her life as well. Serendipitously, while working for Thompson on an ex-pat assignment in Indianapolis, Schiepers happened to see the first episode of *The Apprentice*. "I remember watching it and thinking, 'Oh, if they ever do something like that in Belgium, I might participate.'" The seed was planted, and in 2005, she had her chance and won first place in the show, *Topmanager*. (I'll share more about this in upcoming chapters.)

For others, it seemed to be in their nature to embrace adventure that lured them to the precipice of life. Alex Honnold is one such example. His mother, Dierdre Wolownick, shared in her book, *The Sharp End of Life: A Mother's Story*, that Alex would climb over furniture and anything else in his path as a toddler. "On our big swing set in the backyard, he would stand on a swing, launch himself through the air—what climbers call a 'dyno'…grab a cross bar, and then climb up the thick metal pillars, or feet, of the whole swing set…The activities changed as he grew, but the goal always seemed the same: to get higher. A tree, a wall, a building, everything in his world was a means to get higher."

And the higher he went, the more driven he became, as exemplified in the documentary *Free Solo*, which chronicled his climb without ropes on El Capitan, considered the Everest of California.

And like me, these extreme sports enthusiasts learned lessons during their adventures that influenced many areas of their lives.

Mountains Come in All Shapes and Sizes

This brings me to why I feel called to share the "why" behind this book, *The Precipice of Life: Leadership and Personal Growth Insights from a Mountaineer's Edge*.

It wasn't too long after I climbed a few mountains that I realized the knowledge I acquired on the mountains could be applied to every aspect of my life — as a son, a husband, a father, and a businessman. Commitment, perseverance, humility, flexibility, a positive mindset, and so much more are characteristics we need to possess, whether our challenge is in the boardroom or in the dining room of our family home.

In the coming pages, you'll read stories about my adventures and those of a number of extreme sports athletes who have faced adversity on and off the mountain. Additionally, I've included the wisdom from thought leaders who have their own stories of growth and perseverance throughout their careers. Some of these people profiled within *The Precipice of Life* are Kenton Cool, Eric Weinhenmayer, April Rinne, Nate Klemp, Doug Holladay, and many more, in addition to the ones I've previously mentioned.

In these pages, you'll be guided on an expedition. I'll share some of my mountaineering adventures coupled with my growing awareness of how every challenge I overcame and every inner resource I drew upon during my adventures I carried with me back off the mountain. By reading these accounts and insights, I hope you'll be inspired to inquire how these lessons might apply to your own life.

Here's an overview of each of the chapters you're about to experience:

Chapter 1 — Heeding the Call reflects upon the importance of commitment when the whispers of our souls urge us to embark upon our unique journey through life.

Chapter 2 — Taking the Lead explores the concepts of leadership, mentorship, and building teams.

Chapter 3 — Our Unique Risk DNA dives into the idea that we all have our own risk-tolerance or risk-aversion levels, and we can take steps to build our risk tolerance in our everyday life.

Chapter 4 — Slowing Down & Tuning In highlights the importance of slowing down our pace — on the mountain or off — so we can tap into our intuition's valuable and sometimes life-saving information.

Chapter 5 — Falling is Not Failing reframes the concept of failure and how we are meant to learn from our mistakes rather than fall into a spiral of self-denigration when things don't go as planned.

Chapter 6 — Breaking Down to Build Back Up digs into the sometimes-harsh reality that destruction is often necessary before something new — and often better — can be experienced, whether that's in a relationship or in business.

Chapter 7 — Knowing When Enough is Enough probes the idea that sometimes we need to let go and move on rather than continue in fruitless explorations.

Chapter 8—How to Claim Happiness brings to light the ways we all have control over our own happiness if we choose to embrace this responsibility.

Chapter 9—From Success to Significance emphasizes the importance of impacting the world through our legacies.

Plus, at the end of each chapter, I'll invite you to pause and reflect upon a few questions that will allow you to increase your awareness about your relationships, your business, your happiness, and much more. And so, let's begin.

Reflection

» What mountain do you want to climb?

» Who or what inspires you to take your unique journey?

» What compels you to take on this challenge?

"At the moment of commitment, the entire universe conspires to assist you."

— *Johann Wolfgang von Goethe*

CHAPTER 1

HEEDING THE CALL

The call of the mountains began as a whisper, luring me higher and higher into a journey that I had no clue I'd be taking when I first began climbing Longs Peak in Colorado during college. That whisper became louder when I decided to climb Kilimanjaro when the two men I'd met on that mountain informed me of the challenge of conquering the Seven Summits, of which Kilimanjaro was one.

I knew I had no choice but to make a commitment. And I did. I was in—all in.

Next, I set my sights on Aconcagua in Argentina. I was heeding the call these mountains were sending my way. Then, other peaks followed—Aconcagua, Denali, Elbrus, Vinson Massif, Everest, and K2. Each possessed its own unique characteristics that begged for me to listen, go further beyond the edge of my own comfort zone, and embrace yet another precipice in my own life. Curiosity about what I'd learn and who I'd become with each step on the mountain beckoned me onward and upward.

The Curiosity Gene

Being curious is often the first step to choosing an adventure, whether or not that adventure leads us to the top of a mountain or building a business.

In his book, *The Art of Impossible,* Steven Kotler reported that his research identified five major intrinsic motivators—curiosity, passion, purpose, meaning, and autonomy.

"Curiosity is your basic interest in something, and you get focused for free. That's the big deal. We don't have to work to pay attention. It happens automatically. Curiosity is designed in our biology to be built into a passion in a very specific way," he explained.

"Passion is an internal fuel that's coupled to a problem greater than ourselves," he adds. "Once you have purpose, the system demands autonomy, the freedom to pursue your purpose."

Richard Wiese, host of *Born to Explore* and who in 2002 became the youngest president of The Explorers Club, says anyone with a goal and a dream is sparked by that desire to know more. "If you look at the history of humankind, there was always that one person, whether they came out of a tree or out of a cave, who was curious about what was on the other side of that mountain or valley on the bottom of a lake," he shares.

"It's not having a death wish; it's quite the contrary. It's wanting to live as full a life as possible."
— Richard Wiese

In his career as a television journalist and independent documentary filmmaker, Wiese has encountered many explorers—men and women—who like being out in the field and enjoying new experiences. "It's not having a death wish; it's quite the contrary. It's wanting to live as full a life as possible."

This sentiment is echoed by Nims Purja, the Nepal-born naturalized British mountaineer and a holder of multiple mountaineering world records, including the feat of climbing 14 "Death Zone" peaks (anything over 8,000 meters where oxygen levels are too low for human life) in just six months and six days and beat the previous record of seven years. He says, "I climb so I can live every moment."

As I said in the last chapter, each time I climb, I am reborn, and I come to know more about myself in the process. Earlier in my climbing career, I was looking for goals and accomplishments to add to my resume. Now, I want the journey. I want to help other people. I want to have an impact on the world. I want to know what I'm going to learn about myself. "How am I going to grow?" is a question I ponder whenever I'm presented with an opportunity to stretch myself.

Elizabeth Gould, author of *Feeling Forwards: How to Become the Person Who Has the Life You Want*, says, "The goals we have constantly shift and evolve, and they're impacted by what's happening around us, which in turn affects who we become." Elizabeth, who prefers the term aim over goals, says that pursuing our aims is really one of self-discovery even when we might have attached a specific outcome to our actions.

Alison Levine, a mountaineer and leadership consultant, says, "I enjoy the whole experience of pushing myself. Every day presents such a different type of challenge. I enjoy the unknown. The unknown makes life more exciting."

And I heartily agree. That curiosity about who I might become is woven throughout my life, not only as a mountaineer but as a businessman as well. I've come to see this as living on the precipice of growth—of stepping into the unknown—and that's a place of creativity, innovation, and connection not only with myself but those individuals around me, as well as nature.

Making the Choice

Embarking on adventures — whether in the outdoors, in relationships, or in business — is not something many of us take lightly. Months, even years, of research, contemplation, and consideration go into many of our decisions.

For instance, acclaimed rock climber Alex Honnold studied and climbed El Capitan, which rises 3,000 vertical feet from the floor of Yosemite Valley, for ten years before shedding the ropes for his free solo ascent.

Robie Vaughn says his decision to climb Everest took him years. "And was the hardest part of climbing Everest, much more difficult than anything that I did physically."

Canadian Kathy Kreiner-Phillips, who won the giant slalom at the 1976 Winter Olympics in Innsbruck, Austria, was just ten years old when she made the decision to pursue her dream of going for gold. She recalls her father, who was the doctor for the Canadian Olympic Team, coming home with stories and movies of Nancy Greene winning the gold and silver medals. "I remember sitting on the couch thinking that's what I want to do one day. I didn't tell anyone. I specifically remember saying to myself, 'Okay, I'm going to start my training now,'" she shares.

So, she began training near her family's cottage in Timmins, located in northern Ontario, Canada, by running and balancing on logs. "I was doing whatever I could to take those first steps."

Alex Weber, host of *American Ninja Warrior* and author of *Fail Proof: Become the Unstoppable You*, says our internal workings are what ultimately determine the external results. "You have to have clarity that you want to achieve this milestone more than anything," he explains. "It has to make your heart flare up."

Without that, he says you might not reach that goal. "When you hit the real tipping points, the threshold of frustration, embarrassment, or judgment of the commitment, you're probably going to stop. But you'll keep going if you have that deep, powerful visceral why."

My "why"—to discover more about myself—was the driver when I was climbing K2, and I came face-to-face with death as an avalanche sent rocks the size of bowling balls down the mountain. They fell just five feet from me, and if one had hit me, I would have been decapitated.

Emotions swirled in every cell of my being, and my mind whirled after the danger had passed. I had a decision to make. I could either turn back or continue onward. I calculated the risk. I was feeling confident and not ready to have a setback. I wanted to turn this stumbling block into a stepping-stone. It was just another obstacle to meeting my goal of summiting. And I continued onward.

Jack Canfield, Co-founder of *Chicken Soup of the Soul* and author of *The Success Principles: How to Get from Where You Are to Where You Want to Be*, says, "Sometimes you are going to have to persist in the face of obstacles—oftentimes unseen obstacles—that no amount of planning or forethought could have predicted. Sometimes, you'll encounter what seems like overwhelming odds. And sometimes, the universe will test your commitment to the goal you're pursuing. The going may be hard, requiring you to refuse to give up while you learn new lessons, develop new parts of yourself, and make difficult decisions."

In the end, I decided to keep going because I expected to learn something about the world, my myself, my team members, and the mountain, just as I had on other expeditions.

Alex Weber's choice to pursue becoming a participant in *American Ninja Warrior* was also a visceral why. He had been thinking of himself as a former athlete, having left his position as a Lacrosse Coach at a Division One High School. "For about five years, I treated myself as a former athlete. I drank too much. I ate too much. I sat around too much. My confidence plummeted. I felt pretty worthless," he explains. "Then *American Ninja Warrior* came into my life. It made me feel like I was alive, and I wasn't dying." He was ripe for a change.

Yet, even during the year he trained for *American Ninja Warrior*, he continually checked in with himself and asked: "Do I want to do this?" Then he made the decision real. He contacted the best American Ninja Warriors and asked to train with them.

For Alex showing up and training with the best of the best is an example of diving deep. Diving deep doesn't just correlate with physical feats. "For some people, it might be calling the CEO and asking for a five-minute introduction, or in family life, maybe it's booking an off-the-grid trip with your family to some lake town," he explains. "Diving in the deep end can be gross, messy, and imperfect, but you're in it." That's what counts — being willing to allow curiosity to take you to new places.

Claudie Schiepers, my colleague at DLP Capital, was working as a marketing consultant in Belgium when the theme song for the *Topmanager* captured her attention and prompted her into action. She applied to appear on the show, which, as I said earlier, is the Belgium version of *The Apprentice*. When she was accepted, she quit her job, much to the chagrin of her father. "My dad got really mad. He could not understand that I could give up a job and security. But I knew I had to do it. I also knew I'd figure something out after the competition was over," she explains.

With an innate sense of trust in herself and knowing she had to seize the opportunity, she packed her bags. "Two weeks after being accepted, I was in that house with all the other candidates, and we were filming the episodes. Seven weeks later, I walked out as the winner."

Claudia says it was the feeling of adventure that called to her. "I was in a bad relationship at the time, so it was the perfect escape out of that relationship," she adds. "But there was also a sense of excitement, a sense of trying to do something I hadn't done before. The adventure came at the right time. I was at the right place. Everything kind of clicked. It was perfect."

Sometimes Pain is the Driver

At certain times, individuals need a change in order to grow. Life has become mundane or, in some cases, painful due to toxic relationships or unfulfilling jobs.

Shortly after my first book, *Die Trying*, was published, I received an email from a woman saying that what I'd shared helped her heed the call to go to medical school. In her fifties, she'd been a nurse for her entire career but deeply longed to go further and become a doctor. Her biggest stumbling block was the physical and mental abuse by her husband. "I've always wanted to go back to medical school, but my husband said I wasn't smart enough," she shared. "After hearing you talk and reading your book, I've divorced him. I took the MCAT, and I am starting medical school. I know that I am smart enough."

In my case, the pain of not feeling good enough, stemming from my learning disabilities and being the product of a household with a difficult divorce and the subsequent blending of families, triggered a desire to overcome my weaknesses. Every day in school was fraught with hardship, and I agonized with not one or two mistakes but often countless. There was so much pain that it was often unbearable, and for a time, I buried it, as most people do.

My relationship with my father was complex. His business consumed him, and even when he was home, my parents' challenging relationship and their divorce often overshadowed our home life. After he remarried, his attention was divided even more as my stepmother had children of her own, and they were often present during my visits. I rarely had the opportunity to spend time alone with him. Those circumstances are some of the drivers of my desire to be successful — to finally capture his attention — and feel worthy of his love.

However, I've discovered that behavior is often counterproductive. It created a frenzied, often out-of-balance lifestyle trying to prove my worth to him. Eventually, I realized I had to feel worthy first, which required me to focus on my strengths rather than my weaknesses. To do that, I had to unpack what I call "The Black Box."

It is one of the hardest, if not the hardest, thing I've ever done in my life, and admittedly the unpacking continues. I've suffered doing it, but I knew I had to — and am continually committed to facing those parts of me that lurk in the shadows of my psyche. It's lifelong work. It's a journey. And on the other side of it is freedom. Each time I embrace the courage to look at the sadness, regret, and anger residing inside of me, I become more at peace with who I am. I have the freedom to love myself on a deeper level, and from that space, I'm more available to connect with others. I don't think I ever would have had the relationship I have with my dad now if I hadn't done that work. I don't think I ever would have gotten married. I don't think I ever would have been the dad to my sons that I am today. And even though my business and climbing endeavors often take me far from home, I make a special effort to connect with each of my boys. I never want them to feel "not good enough" and struggle to know that they are worthy of love just by being themselves.

> "Each time I embrace the courage to look at the sadness, regret, and anger residing inside of me, I become more at peace with who I am."
>
> — Bo Parfet

Yet, the mountains provided me with the platform to find that place of "good enough" within me. That arena doesn't offer much room for mistakes if any. In some cases, it could mean the difference between life and death. But jagged peaks and barren valleys have also been where I had the courage to look inside The Black Box and find freedom. That courage to look within takes commitment, not only the commitment to heed the call to climb but also to commit to expanding my awareness of life on and off the mountain.

Lynne Twist & Sara Vetter of the Soul of Money Institute believe that "Genuine commitment comes from the heart and arises from a vision inspired by what's possible…Commitment reorders our actions in alignment with a new future. It is a way of being that informs the direction of our lives, remaining steadfast, even in the face of adversity and challenge…It deepens our trust in ourselves, in life, and brings us vast inner freedom and fulfillment we never even knew was possible."

Resistance to the Call

However, not heeding the call comes with its own level of pain and suffering. Laurie Seymour, the founder of The Baca Institute, who works with entrepreneurs and thought leaders to help them achieve higher levels of personal and professional success, says that once the call has been acknowledged, it can become quite painful *not* to take a step toward heeding it.

"If we're really meant to do something, that call keeps coming stronger and stronger and stronger," she explains. "Our will can be strong, and we can deny it. Life will go in another direction. However, my experience with that is we always have a feeling of missing something. We missed our timing."

Laurie views committing to a calling as the first step of a dance. Dancing requires that we listen to the tune of the music and move accordingly, and to do that, we need to be flexible.

Flexibility is Key

Being attached to specific outcomes and allowing logic to dictate our agenda can be devastating not only to our egos but to our lives. Admittedly, I've erred on the side of logic both on the mountain and in business.

When embarking on a K2 expedition, many climbers will purchase the permits for K2 and Broad Peak, both of which are located in the Karakoram Range. The idea is that many people climb Broad Peak to acclimatize before the ascent on K2. It's also a way to pass the time if the weather on K2 prevents an ascent attempt. In hindsight, my goal was to climb K2, and narrow-mindedly, I didn't see the need to spend the extra money on the Broad Peak permit. I'd already budgeted for K2. Instead of planning for flexibility, my dogged approach was actually a setback. When I arrived at base camp, which serves both peaks, the weather on K2 was not conducive to climbing, so I had to wait it out while other climbers seized the moment on Broad Peak. My inflexibility prevented me from having an experience that might have served me in ways that I will never know.

On the flip side, I called upon my flexibility during the time I worked for my father at MPI Research. We had an agreement where I was to work for him for a year with the objective of increasing revenues in the medical device division. If I were successful, I would be assigned to the senior management role. That year, which was during the second worst economic downturn in history, I increased the revenue in multiple divisions of the company, including the medical device division by 42%. When we discussed the outcome of my efforts, expecting a promotion, my father said he would follow up with me. Three or four months went by with no communication, and when I broached the subject again, he said he needed me in my current position for another year. Rather than leaving the company, I stayed and gave it to him.

Unfortunately, at the end of that year, which experienced another 40%+ growth, it became clear that my father wasn't ready to turn over the reins to his company to me or anyone anytime soon—and perhaps never. He said I needed to win over his senior management team before I would be invited into that circle. I knew that would never happen because they were loyal to my father. I learned a great deal about myself and the business during that time, for which I am grateful. Yet, I knew it was time to move on.

April Rinne, author of *Flux: 8 Superpowers for Thriving in Constant Change*, says, "There are mountains that you pick to climb, like the Seven Summits, and then there are also mountains that simply get thrown in your path."

Sometimes those mountains feel like insurmountable challenges that life throws at us. Then the only way out is through. "For me, this meant there was a combination of mountains I picked to climb. These were full of all kinds of changes and uncertainties and unknowns," explains April. "And there were also mountains that were lobbed right at me, and I had to climb them whether I wanted to or not."

One of those mountains that was lobbed at April was the loss of her parents, who died in a car accident when she was twenty years old. She had no choice but to climb out of the shock and disbelief that she had been orphaned at a pivotal time in her life.

"There's an important distinction even as it relates to change and even if it relates to any individual mountain, literally or figuratively. You can be climbing one mountain," she adds. "But then, as you're summiting that mountain, there can continue to be all kinds of valleys and cliffs and mountains in between."

April recalls a time when she was hiking in the Himalayas some years ago and thought she saw the top of a mountain, which ultimately turned out to be a mere ridge. "I want to underscore the fact that each of those smaller mountains is still a mountain and still a point on one's longer, deeper journey. They are moments of change, and moments of uncertainty, and moments in which there is some kind of flux."

> "A smaller mountain is still a mountain and still a point on the journey."
>
> — April Rinne

Alison Levine's approach to goal setting is always to remain flexible as well. "The goal might have to change when the situation changes. Being able to pivot is key. For me, goals are never hard and fast. Goals are to remain flexible, based on what's going on around me at the time."

Jason Valadao, MD, author of *Exceptional Every Day*, a former Navy pilot, and now a team physician at the United States Naval Academy, says his drive has been a chip on his shoulder, often getting him in trouble. However, his drive has softened since he's learned the value of being flexible and having a backup plan.

Jason, who begins his day with journaling — a habit he began in his childhood — reflects on the backup plan for each day. In essence, he builds flexibility into his schedule. He's witnessed that people get let down when they lose sight of their goals and also because they don't have a backup plan.

"Being in aviation for ten years in the Navy, we always had to plan for contingencies. What if one of our engines went down and we had to land somewhere in the middle of the Pacific Ocean? We had to be ready," he explains.

To be ready in our own lives, we have to know what's right for us and not what's been mandated by others.

Your Goals or Someone Else's

Elizabeth Gould stresses our aims need to be personal and not a goal to satisfy someone else's expectations. She explains with the *Feeling Forwards* process that she uses with her coaching clients, an inner justification for what we want to achieve is crucial. "We all know that fulfilling society's expectations, fulfilling what we think we should be doing, comparing ourselves to others, won't spring us out of bed."

In "The Power of Your Story: Discovering Your Why, Dissolving Your Why Nots," a chapter in the anthology *Ignite Your Leadership: Proven Tools for Leaders to Energize Teams, Fuel Momentum, and Accelerate Results*, my writing partner, Kathy Sparrow, emphasizes the importance of knowing the source of our "why nots" — those objectives we adopt to win others approval, which often prevents us from living in our greatness.

She says, "When we buy into those limiting and marginalizing stories, our souls are in exile. We spend our days worrying about pleasing others rather than doing what's right for us — which ultimately is right for our families, our community, and the world as well. We lose sight of our why — the passion that evokes flow, excitement, and meaning in our lives."

Taking the time to discover our why — and identify our "why nots" is crucial to a meaningful existence.

> "Taking the time to discover our why — and identify our why nots' is crucial to a meaningful existence."
>
> —Kathy Sparrow

Several years ago, I had the opportunity to experience the 5 Why's Exercise, an iterative process developed by Sakichi Toyoda as a problem-solving method and used by Toyota Motor Corporation. This exercise is helpful to identify whether you have an intrinsic desire to reach a goal or perhaps might be unconsciously going along with someone's program that they designed for you.

Here's an example:

Q: Why do you like that watch on your wrist?

A: Well, I just like the look of it. I like how it feels.

Q: Why do you like how it looks and how it feels?

A: Well, you know I always wanted this type of watch when I was younger and when I could afford it, I wanted this watch.

Q: Why did you want to be able to afford it one day?

A: Well, my dad had a similar watch. My grandpa had one too, and if I got this watch, it would make me feel like I made it.

Q: Why did it make you feel like you'd make it?

A: Well, it would make me feel that I wasn't just, you know, kind of worthless or a loser. Right?

Q: What makes you feel worthless?

A: I haven't pursued the business path that my father and grandfather did, and I feel judged about that.

This is a great exercise that can be done with your partner, your colleague, your kids—anyone like it. When I used this exercise, I drilled down into the fear that I might not be good enough. This was a huge awakening for me. That's when I began focusing on my strengths rather than my weaknesses. I had to choose goals that were important to me—and not as a way to win someone else's approval.

Staying in the Comfort Zone

And as we all know, perhaps from our own experiences, most of the time, people stay within their comfort zones, choosing routines and the known of their daily lives. The adage, "the devil we know is better than the one we don't," rings true for many. Unfortunately, this fixed mindset has us buying into the belief that life will suck if we leave what we know. We refuse to believe in possibilities and opportunities that might expand our horizons and enhance our lives in many, many ways.

Robie Vaughn, who is Chairman of Vaughn Capital Partners LLC, which invests in oil and gas and real estate throughout the United States, has witnessed a tendency in people to play it safe. "They tend to stay in the comfort zone," he explains. "People don't really want to put in that extra effort or be that committed to challenges."

He believes that saying "yes" to opportunities is crucial for our evolution, something he discovered for himself after turning his back on an opportunity at a young age. While attending The University of Texas at Austin, he had the desire and passion necessary to walk onto the football team—and he passed it by. "What I didn't realize at that age is that it doesn't matter if you're successful or not. What matters is that you try it. If you're interested in it, you try it. If you're passionate about it, you try it, and you give it your best shot. It doesn't matter if you fail or succeed; what matters is trying and trying with your best ability," he explains.

A few years ago, I had one opportunity to work for The Nature Conservancy in Asia. It was a super-cool offer, but I turned it down. Like many people who are in similar circumstances, I've spent some time wondering what life would be like for me now had I taken that job. One will never know. Instead, I turned my attention to other pursuits and began Denali Venture Philanthropy with my wife, Meredith. I'll share more about this in the last chapter, but our mission is to move a million people out of poverty through investments with impact entrepreneurs, world-changing technologies, and businesses tackling the biggest problems of health, education, and the environment.

Continuous Evolution

One way to step outside the comfort zone is by being willing to be curious and open to personal and professional growth. Richard Wiese admits that his curiosity has evolved. "As I've aged, I've noticed that curiosity has shifted from an outward curiosity to an inward curiosity."

Adding, "The one thing that you can never take away from people is education. That's why I always say to people just keep evolving. I've noticed that it's very easy, especially for males, to get very set in their ways at a certain stage in life. 'This is what I eat on Sundays. This is what I eat on Wednesdays. I go to bed this early.'" Those beliefs are prime examples of a fixed mindset that can only lead to stagnation.

Robie Vaughn echoes a similar sentiment about the need to evolve. "Maybe it's a human trait to nest and to be safe and know what comes tomorrow, the outcome. For example, I have a lot of friends who love the game of golf. Many of those people dream of retiring as early as possible in life and being able to play golf every day.

"I'm not interested in doing that. To me, that feels like having one foot in the grave. I need the challenge. I have an interest in a lot of different subjects," Robie explains. "And that's probably why I'm not very good at any one specific thing because I am interested in a lot of things. I try a lot of things, I experience a lot of things. Curiosity is one the greatest gifts you have, whether it's through reading or having challenging experiences."

> "Curiosity is one the greatest gifts you have, whether it's through reading or having challenging experiences."
>
> – Robie Vaughn

Robie says that the world is continually changing and that we as individuals also need to change, "The key is to embrace that evolution. This is how you grow."

However, not everyone needs to set their sights on the Seven Summits. It's important to identify reasonable goals within our capacity, but that also stretch us outside of our comfort zone. Additionally, it shouldn't be too easy.

Marcus Baur, former Olympic yacht racer and creator of the software Goalscape says, "The average person needs a moderately challenging goal. If it's too challenging, they drop it; if it's too easy, they get bored."

He acknowledges, "There are people who need big hairy audacious crazy goals, but on average, most people need a moderately challenging goal. That's really what triggers them and makes them continue because they enjoy the small wins on the path to something that seems achievable to them."

Whether or not the goals are specific enough to know when we've attained them must be taken into consideration as well. Baur says the research he's accumulated while creating his Goalscape software indicated that sportspeople are motivated on several levels. "From what I've deducted, I assume that sportspeople are more motivated because the goal they're trying to achieve is more visual. Also, they're more in tune with their inner reward system. That's what creates motivation."

He explains, "If you're a mountain climber, it's simple to understand the actual physical goal. You want to go to the summit, and you're either up there, or you're not up there. Everybody gets that, and that triggers our inner reward system."

However, in business, goals are not as motivating because it often revolves around an abstract idea. "Very often, the central goal is becoming better than the competition or increasing revenues by a percentage," Baur explains. "It's not visual in the sense, such as 'I want to get up on K2.' That's so clear and vivid and understandable."

Baur believes that the ambiguity of business goals can be overcome by leadership frequently discussing the goals and being as specific as possible. "How can you give yourself a pat on the back if you don't know whether you made it, right? You know when you made it to base camp, and you know when you made it to the next camp, but in business, often people don't know if they make it or not."

That lack of motivation can be troublesome — and it also can be remedied. Baur holds that high motivation comes from a multilayered goal structure where we're not just trying to achieve one thing; we are actually trying to achieve a couple of things. "When I was twenty years old, I wanted to go to the Olympics. I wanted to prove something to myself. That was a very personal goal. But I also wanted to go to Australia, and I wanted to represent my country, Germany. It was important for me to stand for my region, my city, and my sailing club."

Likewise, Claudia Schiepers decided to join DLP for a new challenge." She admits to becoming complacent in her previous position at Greystone & Co. "It was almost getting too easy. I worked four days a week, making very good money, but I was bored."

For Claudia, adventure doesn't come in the form of climbing mountains, skiing, or jumping out of planes. "I'm very content in my life. I'm very happy with my family, and I don't have a need for constant improvement there," she explains. "But I have it very much at work. I really want to add value. I want to do it right. I want to work hard."

Currently, even with decades of success as an executive, she is pursuing her MBA program at Vlerick Business School — simply because she wants to keep learning.

Sacrifices

Reaching for higher summits on the mountain or in business is not accomplished without some sacrifices. When I trained for K2, I rarely saw my family. I was working 60-70 hours a week and then trained for another 30 hours. My training was intense — and, in my mind, necessary. I was doing cardio four days a week, sleeping in a Hyperoxic altitude chamber, and working out with a training mask that made me look like Darth Vader. On many Thursday nights, I would eat a big meal preparing me for an intense climb on Fridays, where I would deprive myself of food or water for 12-14 hours. On Saturday mornings, I'd engage in another intense workout for hours.

These sacrifices meant I had to embrace the pain — pain that I chose. In my estimation, there are two types of pain in the world. There's the pain of discipline and the pain of regret. One of them weighs a hell of a lot more than the other, that of regret. I'd already had enough of that in my life. The discipline of sacrifice is a much easier pill to swallow. Ultimately, as a parent, I hope that the disciplines I adopt, which often include intermittent fasting even when I'm not actively training for a big climb, are teaching my boys about delayed gratification.

> "There's the pain of discipline and the pain of regret. One of them weighs a hell of a lot more than the other, that of regret."
>
> — Bo Parfet

When I set off for K2, my youngest son was just a few weeks old. My life was clearly out of balance, and I know my schedule affected the household. However, focusing on my goal to climb K2 had to come first. Without that focus, not only the odds of stepping foot on the mountain were slim, and the risk to my safety and that of my team would have been high if I wasn't emotionally, mentally, and physically ready to make the climb.

Marcus Baur also made sacrifices when pursuing his Olympic dream and often heard from his family that they missed having him around. "You need to get very clear if you want to achieve something that you may not have the highest talent for. You've got to be aware that you may have to make some serious sacrifices." He suggests asking yourself whether you want to make sacrifices and have an unbalanced life before committing to a goal.

"Just because you *want* to achieve a goal that *doesn't make it right* to achieve the goal. It has to make sense in a holistic way," he adds. "If you're super, super talented, things may come easy, and you just dance through the whole thing, but that's also not the normal state of affairs."

Marcus also believes periods of imbalance are fine. "But it's important to do that consciously. If done unconsciously, you're headed for disaster."

In my experience, any goal worth achieving is going to require that we endure some pain (often a lot) and demand sacrifice on some level. Whenever we take a stand for something we feel necessary for our well-being, whether that's a physical, emotional, financial, or spiritual goal, there will be a price paid.

I've mitigated the price my boys pay for my absence, whether it's because of climbing or business, by dedicating time to my family through the family board meeting. About once a quarter, I spend four hours with my boys individually. I symbolically put the phone down and turn it off, and even leave it in the car. They get to choose our activity. It's time I devote solely to them, which forges our connection. (In Chapter 8, "How to Claim Happiness," I'll share more of our father-son adventures.)

Passions, callings, and goals always have a cost. It's how we view the sacrifices we make that determines whether we've adopted a fixed mindset or a growth mindset. If we're complaining about what our goal prevents us from doing, then our viewpoint is narrow.

However, if we observe the benefits of our undertakings, then our world expands. I can focus on the time I've missed with my boys, or I can adopt the mindset that I'm setting a good example for them, especially when it comes to pursuing their goals and responsibilities.

This approach to our mindset is referred to as the broaden-and-build-theory of positive emotions and is the foundational work of Barbara Frederickson, Director of the Positive Emotions and Psychophysiology Laboratory (PEP Lab) at UNC-Chapel Hill, Founding Co-Chair of the Association of Positive Emotion Laboratories (APEL), and current President of the International Positive Psychology Association (IPPA).

"The broaden-and-build theory underscores the ways in which positive emotions are essential elements of optimal functioning and, therefore, an essential topic within the science of well-being. The theory, together with the research reviewed here, suggests that positive emotions: (i) broaden people's attention and thinking; (ii) undo lingering negative emotional arousal; (iii) fuel psychological resilience; (iv) build consequential personal resources; (v) trigger upward spirals towards greater well-being in the future; and (vi) seed human flourishing. The theory also carries an important prescriptive message," says Frederickson. "People should cultivate positive emotions in their own lives and in the lives of those around them, not just because doing so makes them feel good in the moment, but also because doing so transforms people for the better and sets them on paths toward flourishing and healthy longevity."

Additionally, every big climb I've ever adopted has made a positive impact through the books I write, the speeches I give, and the money raised for charity. It's never an either-or, but a both-

and. Knowing what truly calls to us, identifying the sacrifices we're willing to make, and acknowledging where we might be holding ourselves back are vital first steps.

Reflection

» What are you curious about?

» What prevents you from committing to taking action toward a goal or an aim?

» What sacrifices are you willing to make to reach your goals?

» If you're not willing to make sacrifices, what's holding you back?

"A leader is one who knows the way, goes the way, and shows the way."

— John Maxwell

CHAPTER 2

TAKING THE LEAD

In 2005, I was at Cho Oyu, in Tibet—the sixth tallest mountain in the world. I planned to be the youngest American to ski down the trail, so at midnight, I began my trek, feeling good and moving at a good pace.

As I looked up at the sky, the stars were so close, and I was so high up. It was almost as if I was looking down at the stars.

After taking in that breathtaking nighttime horizon, I spotted what I believed to be a really bright star, but then realized it was only 300-400 yards away. It wasn't a star it was someone's head torch.

I continued climbing steep rock bands, gaining on the head torch with each step. As I approached this person, I noticed he was leaning against the mountain, sitting on an outcropping of rock. He was holding his open water bottle with an ungloved hand. Then, I noted that his oxygen mask was off, and his head was tilted back. I touched his shoulder, and there was no response. I took off my glove and pushed my hand down his back. He was still warm, and I felt the labored rise and fall of his chest. I secured his oxygen mask and increased the flow to the maximum. All the while, I was talking to him, and he was not reacting.

Most people climb with a patch of their country's flag on their jacket, but he didn't have one. I radioed down to my base camp.

"I found a guy, mid-50s-60s. He is wearing a red jacket, and he is unconscious. What team is he on?" A few moments later, lights start popping up all over base camp, and I hear languages from around the world being spoken, mixed in with the Sherpa dialect. The radio chatter was intense.

Suddenly, this gentleman's head slowly lifted up, and he looked at me and said, "So, how are you?"

I replied, "Well, I'm fine. How are you?"

"Good. I'm just taking a little rest before I keep going," he responded.

I said, "Well, I think I don't know if you're going to be going anywhere soon."

He said, "Well, what do you mean?"

"I found you, and you weren't doing so well." He looked at me and moved his frostbitten hand slightly; then he went back to sleep.

About a half hour passed, and a Sherpa appeared out of nowhere. He had climbed fast and was out of breath. He spoke to me, half in English and half in his native dialect. We carefully engaged in this conversation, mindful to keep our footing on this super steep slope. Then, he pulled a needle out of his jacket, which I first thought was a pen. I wondered, *"Why does he want to give me a pen?"*

I soon realized it was a needle with dexamethasone, which decreases the swelling of the brain and boosts energy. The Sherpa handed me the syringe. I have never given anyone a shot in my whole life. I absolutely hate needles. So, I gave the needle back to the Sherpa. He handed it back to me. We go back and forth five or six times.

Finally, I knew he was going to win this argument.

I looked down at the syringe in my hand and thought, *"Where do I stick him?"* I only had access to this man's neck, so I jabbed him. Very quickly, he became alert.

Soon another Sherpa joined us, and I determined that it was safe to assign the responsibility of this gentleman to the two Sherpas. Even the man agreed.

It was time for me to continue with my climb.

This was a profound moment of leadership for me. In addition to having keen observation skills, which alerted me to this man's presence and condition, I had to embrace the responsibility of providing him with the life-saving injection, which threw me way outside my comfort zone and took a lot of courage. I just had to decide, and sometimes under extreme situations, there are no wrong decisions. Action is required; in this case, the right decision was made, and the man's life was saved.

Before I pursued with my agenda, I ensured that no extra resources were needed to carry this gentleman back down the mountain. I had buy-in from everyone before I continued with my climb.

Some folks might think, "This isn't my problem," and pass on by. But when a situation arises, a leader needs to step up, whether it's in their wheelhouse or not. It doesn't matter if you're a CEO or a janitor; if something spills on the floor, you pick it up, right? A servant leader does what's called of them in the moment.

A mistake I did make was not planning for that contingency. One of my main goals was to be the youngest American to ski that peak. As I approached the summit, I could not carry my skis anymore. I didn't have the energy. I used my reserves to save that man's life. I shoved my skis into the snow, and I summited without them. I did ski down, but from a short distance below the summit.

I could have held regret or been pissed off at this guy, but I wasn't. I practiced acceptance, and I know I made the right move — all the way around.

Trust is Key

When clinging to the side of the mountain and tethered to other climbers, it's vital to trust your teammates — especially the leader. If someone tarnishes that trust, it erodes the team's spirit and ability to rely on one another and often sabotages the success of the mission. The same can be said of any business venture. The leader is responsible for ensuring that trust is established — and maintained at all costs because, without it, the cost could be a life of an individual or the life of a business.

I've had the opportunity to view leadership from several vantage points, and admittedly I wasn't always the best leader, especially when I was young and unsure of myself. I also didn't know how to accept leadership. In my headstrong ways, I usually wanted to do it my way on my time. My ego definitely got in the way a lot, but luckily as I've matured, I've come to know all my personas (the roles I assume in various circumstances) and how to play them to my advantage. I also watch out for how I might sabotage a situation. My leadership skills are on the rise. And like anything else, it's a journey, a path of continuous development.

Who Are You?

As I discovered, a strong leader is firmly grounded in who they are. They know their strengths and their weaknesses and turn to those around them to fill in the gaps. They understand that they don't have all the answers and are willing to admit this.

Pete Winiarski, CEO of WIN Enterprises, says, "Conscious Leaders start by building a conscious awareness of themselves first, and then build a conscious awareness of others around them, including their teams, their peers, and other people in their sphere of influence. When leaders are Conscious of Self, they inspire others by their personal results and style. When leaders are Conscious of Others, they build followership and create a team that is capable of great performance and transforming company results."

The more I came to know myself, especially through my expeditions, the more confident I became in business and in my relationships. I was experiencing more peace and less angst in my daily responsibilities.

> "A strong leader is firmly grounded in who they are. They know their strengths and their weaknesses and turn to those around them to fill in the gaps. They understand that they don't have all the answers and are willing to admit this."
>
> — Bo Parfet

Chander Mishra, MD, an anesthesiologist and real estate investor, has a deep spiritual practice that filters through all areas of his life. He recently shared the idea with me that while climbers are going on their external journey, they're simultaneously going on an inner journey.

"That process starts working right when they start the climb; as they climb, they slowly let go of more of themselves; that's when the flow comes in. Each climb is like shedding their identifications, and that's why they keep coming back," he explains. "While initially when on the summit one becomes aware of knowing something bigger than themselves, it's temporary. Soon the self they identify with — the "I" — dissolves and results in expansion of divine spirit."

That connection with the Divine within us can be palpable, particularly when we step away from the distractions of daily life. The presence one feels when standing on what seems like the top of the world fills me with awe. That experience feeds my soul. And I know others feel the same.

"Climbing is a tool to let go of what binds us," Chander explains. "It allows the individual to see themselves more clearly. They remove a veil."

I must admit that while early on, my ego was often running the show on the mountains as well as in my career and relationships, with each expedition, that which bound me to a fixed mindset began to dissolve. It was a practice of surrender and growing self-awareness that at times was more arduous than climbing in the Death Zone—and it was just as rewarding, if not more so.

And yet, Chander says, "Most people are not fearful of losing the ego self. Most people are most afraid of gaining that power."

With power comes responsibility. We are no longer able to act unconsciously without the ramifications to our relationships, our businesses, and even our health and well-being as individuals.

Pete Winiarski says, "As leaders build a more conscious awareness of themselves, they can become more effective. They get great personal results in a way that helps them to manage stress and helps them experience more inner peace and joy in the process. They display a higher level of self-confidence that translates to the other people around them."

Be Humble

It wasn't long before I witnessed that there was always someone better than me at mountain climbing and business. If you don't acknowledge that, then your ego can "kill you," figuratively or literally. Being humble allows us to be in a position to grow and learn from those around us.

One of my mentors said his best teacher was his young child. Children are always in the present moment and don't really worry about the past or the future. I can see that in my boys. Animals are the same. They are always in the moment, comfortable in their own skin. They're not worried about what they look like to others. They express their unique selves with ease.

Unfortunately, most of us aren't that comfortable with who we are. We worry about how others perceive us, and then when we do make mistakes, we draw out our cards for the blame game, and our defenses run wild. Our pride takes us down the wrong path, where if anyone was tempted to look upon us as a leader, our image might be quickly tainted.

Humility is called for. Attaining a high degree of humility takes practice. Without that attribute, we're driven by the logic of ego, and that's not always the best place to make decisions.

Dr. Katie Ervin, CEO and founder of Catalyst Development, says, "Leadership is a responsibility, not a privilege. We succeed in leadership when we are humble enough to admit our mistakes and understand we are only successful with having a strong team around us. We cannot know everything about everything. Build a strong team and listen when your team is honest with you."

Communication Is Key

While it's important to be well-versed in your area of expertise, it's not your place to do all the talking or to know all of the answers. In fact, it's important to ensure that everyone is included in the conversation and that all opinions are heard. Listening to others establishes a connection and allows individuals to feel seen and heard for who they are.

Yet, it's vital to move beyond mere words. The art of observation is essential. We not only need to be listening to the words but also be reading the signs of what's being said in-between the words—and sensing the energy of the exchange.

"Most of us tend to think of communication purely in terms of the words, tone, gestures, and facial expressions we use to get our message across," says Maryanne O'Brien, author of *The Elevated Communicator: How to Master Your Style and Strengthen Your Well-Being at Work.* "There's a whole communication system that operates just below our conscious level of awareness that's always sending and receiving messages between us...Every thought, intention, and emotion carries a frequency that moves through this field of energy. This means that you're always sending messages to others—messages that you may not even be aware of—that influence how they feel, think, and behave, and visa versa."

> "There's a whole communication system that operates just below our conscious level of awareness that's always sending and receiving messages between us."
> — Maryanne O'Brien

According to Maryanne, we often communicate unconsciously without considering the effect we're having on others. I notice that when I haven't taken care of myself, especially with my nutrition and exercise, I'm not at my best in expressing myself or even listening. In fact, I'm not being responsible with the energy I bring into the room or a conversation. That will affect the outcome of the exchange, and often negatively.

"We must stop to think about how we affect the people around us," says Alex Weber. "We have a responsibility to maintain a positive attitude and resilience. We must take care of our energy." Showing up as our best selves ensures that everyone is honored and respected.

Additionally, fine-tuning our listening skills provides an opportunity to learn and possibly find solutions to problems that we weren't capable of seeing on our own.

What's Your Communication Style?

Knowing our communication style is key. Maryanne O'Brien has identified four communication styles: Expressive, Reserved, Direct, and Harmonious.

From her research, she discovered that most of us are Expressives (37%), and these people "love to share their ideas and perspectives about everything." Additionally, she finds that "Establishing a personal connection drives the way they engage and allows them to build close working relationships and extensive networks."

Individuals with a Reserved communication style, representing 25% of the population, "are confident in their abilities and the most comfortable of all the styles in forming an opinion in the moment."

Direct communicators rank at 22% and "value communication that's substantive, brief and produces results...and they're often responsible for keeping people on task. They're built for achievement and love to get right down to business in all forms of communication."

Lastly, Harmonious communicators make up 16% of the population. They are best described as "natural diplomats...they're often the glue that holds teams together and keeps the work flowing. They value creating supportive working relationships and protect them by keeping the peace."

Maryanne says that in order to be effective, we need to be intentional in our communications rather than operate on autopilot. She adds, "More often than not if you think about your autopilot as your default, you'll notice that when you're under stress, it brings out all the shadow aspects. It is us at our worst, and sometimes you're aware of it, and sometimes you're not."

"We must stop to think about how we affect the people around us," says Alex Weber. "We have a responsibility to maintain a positive attitude and resilience. We must take care of our energy."

I happen to be primarily an Expressive and secondarily Direct. I notice that when I'm tapping into the qualities of collaboration, curiosity, and openness, I'm able to connect deeply with those I'm in a relationship with—either personally or in the business world. However, when I've let a busy schedule take away from my self-care, I can be more than a nuisance to those around me. In fact, I can be downright nasty—in other words, too direct. And when that happens, patience goes out the window.

To reset, I have to put myself first and then take a deep breath to cultivate patience in my interactions with those around me.

"We have to cultivate an inner willingness to have the patience to be fully present to recognize what someone else needs and do it without judgment," says Maryanne. "You don't change who you are, but you flex a little bit."

Giving Feedback

Learning to give feedback was another one of my life lessons, especially with people I care about, and I see they're either not taking care of themselves or are in bad relationships. My natural inclination would be to jump in and give advice—unsolicited. One mentor said to me, "Bo, you only have one or two silver bullets to use with a relationship, and you better be really careful in how you use those silver bullets."

One time, I used one of those silver bullets unwisely. My sister, Emily, married a guy, and my suspicion was they weren't a good match. Instead of me supporting her and staying out of their business, I decided to tell her that they probably weren't the best fit and likely wouldn't last. For a few years, she didn't talk to me, and I lost that connection. They ended up getting divorced, and my sister and I reconnected. But those are years I can't get back. So I wasted a silver bullet, and I regret that I did.

Building Trust

Effective communication also requires that there be trust. At times that trust is eroded when our patience wanes, and we haven't considered how our actions and attitudes might be affecting situations.

"When other people need you, you become your best. In a brass-tacks way, be dependent on being needed. Be relied on," says Alex Weber. "Put yourself in positions where other people are saying, 'I need this from you. I'm depending on you.'" Alex believes that if we do that, the best will come out in us.

Claudia Schiepers advocates having fun and relaxing even when the stakes are high, something she gleaned from her participation in *Topmanager*. "I noticed that the people who lasted the longest were the people who could separate the competitive tasks from our friendship. During the day, we were competitors, and, in the evenings, we were friends," she explains. "We were living in the same house. We needed to get along."

Trust is also rebuilt when one is vulnerable. I know in my deepest moments of owning up to my mistakes and exhibiting vulnerability, especially with Meredith, that that there is a pathway to regain the trust I have eroded.

"You have to be willing to open up again and be willing to put yourself in a place where you may feel the pain of being disrespected," Maryanne says.

The key to building trust and keeping it is to communicate "above the line" with curiosity, sincerity, and honesty, to name a few. Avoiding "below the line" qualities such as judgment, complaining, and blaming are vital as well.

Building Trust Through Conscious Communication

Responsible	Listens	Curious	Respectful
Sincere	Engaged	Patient	Addresses issues
Honest	Open	Caring	Resolve conflicts
Blame	Tune-out	Interrupt	Manipulative
Complain	Negative	Disrespectful	Ignore tension
Gossip	Judgmental	Argumentative	Avoid conflict

Courtesy of Maryanne O'Brien

"If you get everyone to agree to operate above the line, you can avoid 90% of the issues. It's just whenever we slip below that, or we trigger someone inadvertently, that difficulties ensue," says Maryanne. "When you're in a life and death situation, and you need everyone standing above the line."

As I experienced more times than I care to remember, past experiences often trigger our emotional responses and taint our communication. More than once, I've said things I wish I hadn't because, in retrospect, the situation reminded me of my childhood wounds.

Maryanne reminds us that people are often doing their best, and if someone gets triggered, it's a sign that they haven't addressed a wound.

And to instill hope, trust, and optimism in those around us demands that we up the game on our communication skills. It's complicated to develop because people are complex, and but it requires us to evolve and grow.

A typical practice before any expedition is to have multiple calls to discuss logistics, get to know one another, and address any other issues that might come up in the preparation phase. These calls also serve to break the ice between individuals who may not know one another very well, if at all. If you've seen *Top Gun: Maverick*, you may remember that before a critical mission, Maverick has the crew on the beach playing football. That initially drew the ire of his commanding officer, but the day at the beach cemented a strong bond between the individuals, a critical act, especially since their lives were in danger.

Choosing a Mentor

Not only do we have to be cognizant of our own leadership style, but when we are seeking mentoring, it's important to choose wisely. I've sought out mentors throughout much of my adult life — in mountaineering, business, and relationships. At times, I was blinded by what I perceived to be their genius, but in the end, I discovered that their charismatic overtures merely shrouded overblown egos.

I've discovered over time that discernment is vital, or we'll be led down the wrong path, or worse, develop a dependency on individuals whose interest isn't in helping us gain knowledge and grow personally or professionally. Some mentors are master manipulators, and they hook us with their linguistic skills and charisma and the image they portray to the world. But in the end, they're not dedicated to serving others. Their focus is on feeding their own egos.

We need mentors who are vested in our individuation, just like a good parent who wants to see us succeed in the world by expressing our unique genius. These individuals must be grounded in their own being, comfortable in their own skins, and secure enough in themselves that they aren't emotionally attached to their clients or their role in their client's life. Unfortunately, many mentors may form an unhealthy attachment to their clients to have a sense of their own accomplishment. In essence, they're looking for something that they haven't received in their own development.

A word to the wise: place your body, mind, and soul in good hands, and choose mentors whose values match your own. Do your research and thoroughly vet them, just as one might research the corporate culture of a company before applying or accepting a job offer. Prior to committing to an expedition team, a business coach, or relationship expert, ask questions, tap into your intuition (more on this in later chapters), and be ready to walk away if you feel yourself acting to win their approval.

Build a Strong Team

Most expeditions require that we spend not days but weeks away from our businesses and our family. Extreme environments bring out the best in people and bring out the worst in people. I've witnessed both and deemed it essential to choose team members who were physically, emotionally, and spiritually mature enough to be able to navigate the stresses that often appear unexpectedly or grow over time during a climb.

Whenever I'm building an expedition team, I assess the experience level, and 9 times out of 10, I go with people who are the most experienced. I also evaluate their egos and ability to be team players. Having a medical professional is also key. I even go as far as doing background checks on all the possible participants of the adventure.

Katie Ervin says, "Strong teams have people from all different backgrounds, experiences, and skills. If we surround ourselves with people just like us, we run the risk of living in an echo chamber. In order to have a well-rounded team, we need people who can fill in gaps. "Thinking that you are a 'team' because you all work in the same area or for the same department is flawed."

Having diverse teams in the workplace has a multitude of benefits. According to Jane Stevenson, Vice Chair of Korn Ferry, and Evelyn Orr, head of CEO and Executive Assessment, "A landmark Korn Ferry study reveals key insights on what traits put women ahead despite diversity issues that still persist." In particular, they discovered that women "were driven by both a sense of purpose and achieving business results. More than two-thirds of the women interviewed and assessed said they were motivated by a sense of purpose and their belief that their company could have a positive impact on the community, employees, and the world around them. Nearly a quarter pointed to creating a positive culture as one of their proudest accomplishments."

Companies with diverse teams also tend to be more profitable. According to Emma Hinchliffe who wrote the article, "Companies with More Women at the Top Fared Better During the Pandemic" for *The Broadsheet, Fortune's* newsletter for and about the world's most powerful women, "There are plenty of arguments for why companies should make diversity—at every level, but especially at the top—a priority. But since we live in a capitalist society, the rationales that really get executives' attention tend have something in common: money."

She cited research from BoardReady and reported that "According to its new analysis of data from S&P 500 companies, there's a strong correlation between board diversity and revenue growth during the pandemic. Here are a couple of the top-line findings, which compare revenue from 2019 and 2020:

- Companies where women held more than 30% of board seats outperformed their peers in 11 of 15 sectors.

- Companies with at least 30% of seats held by non-white directors saw year-over-year revenue grow by 4%. Those with less racially diverse boards had a revenue decline."

Don Wenner, Founder & CEO of DLP Capital (and my boss) is a Level 5 Leader, who knows the importance of building a diverse team—and acknowledges the necessity of having powerful women leaders in the mix. There are four women in senior leadership at DLP. He is great at putting people in the positions to use their superpowers. For example, some of my superpowers are relationship building. This helps us find good real estate operators with which to deploy debt and equity, good speakers for our events, and potential investors.

Don's Level 5 attributes are consistent with other leaders who transform good companies into great ones. In the *Harvard Business Review* article, "Level 5 Leadership: The Triumph of Humility and Fierce Resolve," Jim Collins writes that a Level 5 leader is "an individual who blends extreme personal humility with intense professional will." They also get to know the people they work with personally. They invest in them and their families. There was a husband and wife with four kids in our community. They were a dual-income family. The husband tragically died, and the wife couldn't afford their mortgage payment, so Don bought the house for them.

Erik Weihenmayer has always prided himself on building effective teams, knowing that as a blind climber a team was essential. "As a blind person, a lot of the things I do are required to be 'team' sports. I ski with a guide out in front of me, yelling instructions. I tandem bike, so somebody is piloting my bike. When I'm paragliding, somebody is on the ground talking to me via radios," Erik says. "I think this is one of the hidden gifts of blindness. You get to connect with good people, and then you put your life in their hands. They put their life in your hands, as well, and you're trusting each other. It's really beautiful."

When a cause or a mission becomes a shared vision, magic happens, and that's the outcome of building a strong team. Even if one member will receive the most accolades, be it an expedition leader or the head of a department, developing that sense of oneness allows for greater possibilities, often more than we can imagine in the beginning stages of any adventure.

During one of his expeditions, Erik explained that each morning his team would meet over coffee, and his team leader, Pascuale a/k/a PV, shared a dream that he had on several occasions. "He would say, 'I had that dream again, and it's you and me climbing over the Hillary Step, arm in arm, moving together, and we'd summit. He said that he'd end up crying because if he could do that, it would be the hardest thing he'd ever done," Erik shares. "I love that his ego was saying, 'Hey, I want to devote my energy to this pioneering project. I think that's why 19 out of 21 of us summited. Every person wanted to be there—each knowing that they had an essential piece to contribute— to be a part of this thing that had never been done before. Ultimately, I don't think they gave up themselves to help me. No, they gave *to* themselves by helping me."

Surround Yourself with Genius

We grow personally and professionally by committing to continuous learning. We do this through podcasts, books, and our association with high-performing individuals who could make valuable contributions to our lives, if we're willing to ask.

Belonging to professional groups is one way to move the needle on our growth. As Chief Growth Officer for DLP and throughout my mountaineering career, I've been involved with a multitude of teams and discovered what makes these groups a success. Ideally, the group should revolve around "three or more people connected through shared identity, common purpose, and mutual influence. Different groups can have different characteristics or serve different purposes. A team of professional college counselors, a campaign team for a state senator, or a group of professional writers all represent examples of groups with different identities, structures, interaction patterns, and sizes," as I shared in the Corporate Communications for RUSH PR Wire.

However, "informational diversity is key. When diverse people are brought together to solve a problem, they come in with different perspectives, opinions, and information."

Own Your Wisdom

Being confident is vital for leading a team, protecting a family, or saving a company from financial ruin during a challenging economy. Years of experience build our wisdom. Combine that with tapping into our intuition and our intellectual knowledge, we can make a big difference in most situations.

> "Whether clinging to a glacier or facing difficult decisions in your business, it's important to be confident that your experience has put a vast amount of 'stock' in your bank account."
>
> — Bo Parfet

"Cumulative knowledge makes you more decisive. When you're younger, you're always sort of wondering, 'Is this the right decision?' 'Am I picking the right foods, the right this, the right that,'" shares Richard Wiese. "And it gets to a point, even when you're leading expeditions and when you're leading a group of people, *that you just know that you're making the right decisions and that you're making the best decision with the information on hand.*

"It's because you've gotten out of your head and stopped questioning, 'What are people going to think if we do this or that?'

Once the ego leaves, you're able to observe what's going on. The mind and the eyes are just this incredible computer that's able to assimilate a lot of information rather rapidly."

Whether clinging to a glacier or facing difficult decisions in your business, it's important to be confident that your experience has put a vast amount of "stock" in your bank account.

Richard adds, "Everybody talks about survival skills. And I always say a really good explorer isn't somebody who's able to battle the waves and storming seas. It's somebody who sees dark clouds on the horizon and says, "Let's get to a safe port."

A good leader knows when to take risks and knows when enough is enough, concepts that I'll dive into in the coming chapters.

Reflection

>> How would you describe your communication style at its best and worst?

>> When have you experienced a lack of trust in others?

>> How can you own more of your own leadership qualities?

"Don't listen to others. You need to take chances, and you need to take the risk sometimes in order to make things happen for yourself."

— Nims Purja, Nepalese Mountaineer

CHAPTER 3

OUR UNIQUE RISK DNA

Carstensz Pyramid, located in Papua, Indonesia, was the expedition where I was faced with numerous risks that, when I look back, still make my skin crawl. Cannibalism, sociopolitical unrest, and the overt presence of the military known for their human rights violations were present—all of that even before the climb began, one that posed multiple challenges and moments of extreme trepidation.

During that adventure, I was taking the lead with fellow-climber Max Chaya from Lebanon when I came face-to-face with the most harrowing experience of my climbing career thus far. Max and I were securing and replacing ropes that had definitely seen better days and which were extremely dangerous for our three fellow teammates who followed closely behind. The guide on the trip was Christine Boskoff, the owner of Mountain Madness, who unfortunately was killed about a year after this climb in an avalanche.

At the most dangerous point in the climb, we had to navigate a V-shaped notch, rappelling down a 40-foot slope, and then climb up the inverted wall on the other side of the gap—with a nearly 2,000 vertical drop on both sides of us. Normally, 40 feet is no big deal. But the ropes here weren't any less questionable than the ones we had earlier encountered. To make matters worse, we were the beneficiaries of a steady mixture of rain and snow. That put me on edge, really on edge, especially after Max failed at his first attempt to ascend the wall. I seriously considered calling off the climb, but I continued—as did the tests to my mettle. A few feet off the ground, I found myself dangling over that 2,000 vertical drop after a gust of wind blew me off the wall. Fearing for my life and convinced I would never see my family and friends again, I prayed that the jagged rocks would not slice the rope and send me plunging to my death.

Thankfully, the wind died down, and I was no longer swinging over the precipice. After catching my breath and slowing my heartbeat, I resumed my ascent—more focused and committed than ever to reach the summit.

Built for Risk

Obviously, climbing the Carstensz Pyramid involved great risk, a risk that some would find absolutely insane. The fact is that some of us are built to take more chances. But for others, picking up a phone to ask someone out on a date or inquire about a job might elicit similar reactions to what I experienced at the end of that rope. They break out in a cold sweat just thinking about making a phone call. Then there are the foolish risk-takers who endanger others because of unresolved issues stemming from childhood.

When I was in my youth, I did some crazy things. At sixteen, I was struggling with all of my perceived difficulties, and I had no channel to process them. I didn't feel seen or heard by people close to me. Subconsciously to gain attention, I would pull some stupid stunts that not only put me in danger but could also potentially harm others. One such act, I repeatedly tried. There was an intersection near my home, and I would intentionally run the stop sign after determining whether or not a car was approaching the intersection on the highway by peering through an opening in the trees. Think of it as a variation of playing chicken. When I made it through the crossroads, I felt more alive. That desire for excessive risk continued into my twenties when I drove a Ferrari at harrowing speeds with police on my tail during the Gumball 3000, a "rally" that took participants from New York to California.

I realize now because of some underdeveloped relationships in my life, I hadn't developed my own sense of self. A part of my growth was hindered by our inadequate father-son relationship. Without that strong bond, I didn't feel safe in my youth. Thankfully, no one was harmed by my childish antics.

> "What I've come to understand is that many mountaineers live somewhere between life and death — knowing that death follows us up every trail. We accept it."
>
> — Bo Parfet

However, while I take fewer risks now that might put others in danger, as I stated in *Die Trying*, "I feel most alive in high-pressure situations with fire-drill deadlines, stretching my physical, emotional, and mental limits to the max. It's hardly surprising that I'm drawn to both mountaineering and business environments. Unlike people who lead structured lives, I have a tolerance for the unknown, for change, even for panic." These are the ingredients that keep me going, even after nearly being blown off the side of a mountain or taking on business endeavors without guarantees of success.

In essence, I'm capable of taking risks in the adventure world that most people won't even consider, as do many of my peers. What I've come to understand is that many mountaineers live somewhere between life and death — knowing that death follows us up every trail. We accept it. We shake hands with the situations and people who want to kill us and walk past them to continue our journeys, our explorations, our adventures.

Nate Klemp, co-author of *Start Here: A Groundbreaking, Science-Based Program for Emotional Fitness*, is a former Stanford-Harvard-Princeton trained philosophy professor. His expertise is in weaving together ancient and modern wisdom to enhance individual well-being. His studies of the Stoics, Plato, and Socrates, among others, led him to the understanding that "When death is front and center in our consciousness, there's a freshness to how we live life."

He explains, "The awareness of death brings with it the awareness of life. And the denial of death brings with it this kind of numbed-out experience of life where we're just kind of going through the motions living with this assumption that everything is just going to stay like this forever, and then we experience terrible suffering."

Risk is a part of everyone's life to some degree. Whenever anyone stretches the boundaries of their current situation and capacities, there is an element of risk — whether we're climbing a mountain, contemplating marriage, embarking on a new business venture, or even taking up a new hobby. Accepting that risk is inherent in everything we do prevents us from becoming static and caught in a prison of our own making. Our mental, emotional, and spiritual well-being requires cultivating risk in our lives. That's what keeps us growing. In fact, it may be that embracing risk is what keeps us alive — even in the face of death.

> "The awareness of death brings with it the awareness of life."
>
> — Nate Klemp

David Dobbs, who wrote the article "Restless Genes" for *National Geographic,* says, "Researchers have repeatedly tied the variant, known as DRD4-7R and carried by roughly 20 percent of all humans, to curiosity and restlessness. Dozens of human studies have found that 7R makes people more likely to take risks; explore new places, ideas, foods, relationships, drugs, or sexual opportunities; and generally, embrace movement, change, and adventure. Studies in animals simulating 7R's actions suggest it increases their taste for both movement and novelty. (Not incidentally, it is also closely associated with ADHD)."

The ADHD Connection

Many executives and entrepreneurs, like myself, have dyslexia and/or ADHD and are held in high regard for the benefits to society as a result of their risk-taking measures. People like Bill Gates, Richard Branson, Jim Carrey, Howie Mandel, and Walt Disney are among the more successful people who have used their learning differences to their advantage. Instead of a curse, as I once believed, I now see that ADHD is a blessing—as do so many others.

"Many successful and unsuccessful entrepreneurs have ADHD. Big names in every field, really, because they're relentless in their pursuit of the new and want to make a change in the way things operate," says John Ratey, MD, co-author of *ADHD 2.0: New Science and Essential Strategies for Thriving with Distraction—from Childhood through Adulthood.*

"They're the ones who say the emperor has no clothes and ask, 'Why are we doing it this way? This is dumb. Let's do it this way instead.' And this leads to innovation and change in our culture," he adds. "People with ADHD are incredibly sensitive and can make very good partners if they sustain their focus on any of the partnerships, both in business and personally."

Richard Branson, who has joined forces with the organization, Made by Dyslexia, adds, "Dyslexic Thinking is a skill that can give you the edge at work: you're likely to have strong problem-solving skills, great imagination, and creative, big-picture thinking." Worth noting is that LinkedIn now has a skill category for Dyslexic Thinking.

He says, "I'm proud to be a dyslexic thinker, and I have used it to my advantage to shape the Virgin brand. It wasn't until I dropped out of school at 16 that I was able to cast my lack of interest in mental arithmetic, my wandering mind, and short attention span in an entirely new light. I recognised these were actually the result of epic imagination. Where others saw problems, I was able to see solutions. Insurmountable challenges became endless opportunities. I was able to easily simplify things and see the bigger picture."

> "We're seekers. We're explorers. We accept risk as a part of the experience."
> — Bo Parfet

Jessica Glazer, a contributor to HuffPost who wrote "ADHD Can Be A CEO's Secret Superpower," compiled a list of eight traits that those with ADHD possess, and risk-taking is one of them. "People with ADHD have no time to think and ponder an idea because if they do, they will forget about it and never make it happen. The person with ADHD is a risk-taker, as it really is now or never!"

Expanding Your Horizons

With or without the risk gene, or ADHD, many believe we were born to explore. Douglas Holladay, the author of *Rethinking Success: Eight Essential Practices for Finding Meaning in Work and Life,* says, "We need to rediscover and delight in risk. It will enliven us and engender a sense of confidence and wonder...That doesn't necessarily mean we must take a big ugly leap of some sort. We can develop a habit of risk-taking in small ways. We then taste the benefits and expand our scope of activity."

One exercise that might be helpful in expanding your risk tolerance would be to think back to something you wanted to do in your youth but didn't, perhaps out of fear, or you were told you weren't good enough to try it. For instance, I always wanted to develop my skill in photography and snorkeling. I've embraced both as a way to eradicate that notion of "I can't."

As I've said before, I'm more alive, fulfilled, and happy when I've taken risks and explored different reaches of the earth and depths of myself. I'm not alone.

"Truly happy people seem to have an intuitive grasp of the fact that sustained happiness is not just about doing things that you like. It also requires growth and adventuring beyond the boundaries of your comfort zone. Happy people are, simply put, curious," says Robert Biswas-Diener and Todd B. Kashdan in the *Psychology Today* article "What Happy People Do Differently."

Yet, modern life keeps us safe and insulated from a desire to take risks. We've grown accustomed to our connectivity and our routines. The noise of our lives drowns out that desire to be curious and explore.

My friend, Kenton Cool, who has climbed Everest sixteen times, believes, "As mountaineers, we face death every time we step foot on the mountain. And in reality, every time we step foot out of our beds in the morning, we come closer to death. But most of us don't think about that. If we did, we'd make better choices. We'd live bigger lives, leaving behind the small, safe lives that many of us were taught to live by our parents and grandparents."

Playing small keeps us safe. When we stay within the confines of our comfort zones, we don't allow our greatness to come forth into the world, and in doing so, we're not leaving a lasting impact on the world. Ultimately, we're not really alive. We're going through the motions, checking off boxes, tending to tasks on our to-do lists — lists often created for us by others.

Kenton, whose adventures have been chronicled in his book, *One Man's Everest: The Autobiography of Kenton Cool,* believes that our Western society doesn't allow the majority of us to face our mortality. "We were not encouraged to push ourselves to the edge. We don't necessarily need to stare death in the face, but we can go out for our 10k run in the morning and push ourselves further, even to the point where we think our lungs are literally about to come out of our chests."

The Relationship with Death

Jamie Wheal, author of *Recapture the Rapture: Rethinking God, Sex and Death in a World That's Lost Its Mind,* discovered that the action sports enthusiasts in ocean or mountain communities have an ongoing relationship with death. "There's more depth, and there's more dignity. They have a relationship with Kali, the destroyer. Mother Nature has fangs, and relating to that, living on that sharp edge, is without a doubt part of what makes people in those communities that much more alive," he says.

In my own experiences, when I'm in a life-and-death situation, I am in the moment. I'm more present. And I'd say happier. That cup of tea I'm sipping after a day of climbing becomes precious.

While I'm in the routine of my "civilized" life, I hardly remember tasting my morning coffee. Thankfully, when we're out of our comfort zones, time slows down. I've learned to appreciate the little things in life. I reflect upon my role as a husband and a father. I think of ways I can enhance my relationship with my wife and my sons. Without those life/death epiphanies, I would go through life half asleep.

Ultimately by facing death, Jamie concludes that we become twice-born. He claims that our first birth was never by choice. "It's really just the accident of a male and a female getting together, who we now call our parents. We were in this warm, wonderful womb, and we get spat out into a cold and harsh world," he says.

> "Ultimately by facing death, we become twice-born."
>
> — Jamie Wheal

Additionally, the initial birth trauma is what many of us seek to escape because we never gave consent. "We do that with drugs. We do that by seeking sex. We do that with online shopping, social media, and virtual reality games. We do anything we can to skirt this human condition," Jamie explains. "However, throughout all traditional cultures, there have always been death and rebirth initiations. Some of them were warrior trainings like the Spartan. Some of them were mystical initiations like the rites of Eleusis."

Mountaineering has been my rite of passage. As I've said before, each time I return from an expedition, from the precipice of life, I feel more alive and, in a sense, reborn. Kenton shares similar thoughts. "I come back from expeditions, and I've made pledges to myself. I'm going to be a better husband, father, and leader. And I ask those around me to hold me accountable."

Jamie Wheal says, "The courting of the death experience and to come back from it is fundamentally necessary to choose life. It's essentially the hero's journey which is evident in so many tales known to us—Ebenezer Scrooge and his Christmas morning epiphany, Jimmy Stewart in *It's A Wonderful Life*, Dorothy and the Wizard of Oz, Jonah and the belly of the whale."

In some ways, being the progeny of successful businessmen who took risks, I've been lucky. I've seen my father and grandfather pour their hearts and souls into businesses that have soared and failed. They set the stage for me to take my own risks. While my mountaineering adventures differ in some ways from theirs, that ability to acknowledge and accept risk as a part of any new venture has woven its way into my business and personal life. I'm able to assess situations and identify the controllable risks and, in many but not all cases, create strategies to navigate the uncontrollable risks.

Controllable and Uncontrollable Risks

Robie Vaughn ventures into his endeavors, whether it's an investment or mountain climbing, cognizant of the fact that there are controllable risks and uncontrollable risks. He believes most of our influence lies with the controllable risks; however, there are steps that can be taken to reduce the uncontrolled risks as well.

"In business and investing, there are multidimensional risks in every deal. The sponsor may be the most significant risk of all. You can have a brilliant idea and perfect timing. If the sponsor is not executing, he's not a good leader, and he's not experienced, in alignment with partners, mature and humble, it may not work."

As I shared earlier, Robie is an accomplished mountaineer whom I first met on Everest in the Khumbu Icefall and again at Camp IV at 26,000 feet when he poked his head in my tent. Here, too, he took steps to mitigate his risks during his climb by putting together his own team, thus further controlling many controllable risks and possibly influencing some of the uncontrollable risks.

"One reason I decided that I would put my own team together was so that I would not be one of the 90-95+ percent of teams on the mountain that were made up of 10-12 or 14-16 people. You can only go as fast as the slowest person on a rope team. Then if someone gets injured or sick, one of the strongest guides must take them down the mountain. That increases the risk for everybody else. These are not isolated risks. These are compounding risks," he shares.

"And so," Robie adds, "I questioned: How do I influence those types of risks? I came to the conclusion that I needed to put my own team together, knowing that I'm the weakest link in the chain. And I had enough experience and confidence in myself that I could make a go of this."

He chose two Sherpas with significant experience to help control the risks. His lead Sherpa had previously summited Everest nine times. And the Sherpa who would climb behind him had been a high-altitude Sherpa for a number of years.

Robie summitted Mount Everest the day after me in 2007, on a clear and calm day, wherein he hit three golf balls off the summit and later contributed his club to the United States Golf Association archives.

Dierdre Wolownick, who at sixty-six became the oldest woman to climb El Capitan, says she is not a risk-taker. Nor does she caution, is her son, Alex Honnold. "He knows exactly what he's going to do with his fingers, with his toes, with everything. It's all planned out. Successful climbing is all about mitigating those risks," she explains. "There's always stuff that can happen—a hold can break, an eagle can fly at you, scare you, and you'll fall off. But as much as possible, climbing is not about embracing risk but doing away with it."

Kathy Kreiner-Phillips, a Canadian Alpine Skier who won the Olympic Gold in the 1976 Winter Games, believes risk-taking is more of an innate behavior that we're born with. "I'm probably not as much of a risk-taker, so everything would have to be calculated out ahead of time as well. The more you know the level of risk that's involved, the more you can plan and calculate."

Erik Weihenmayer, who has been blind since he was fourteen years of age and excels in rock climbing, mountaineering, kayaking, and other sports, has never seen himself as somebody walking the edge of death. "Blind is fine, blind and stupid… is fatal," Erik jokes. While many perceive his feats as reckless, he insists that is extremely calculated.

Like Alex Honnold and Dierdre Wolownick, he believes preparation is key. Weihenmayer speaks of engineering an expedition forward with systems, strategies, and tools, including a well-prepared team for minimizing that risk.

What Keeps Us from Exploring

Richard Wiese holds that people can explore at different levels. We don't all need to be hanging out in the Death Zone. Equally important is for those of us who favor extreme sports to refrain from judging people whose idea of adventure is going out on a rainy day to walk through a local town park. "Everybody has different levels of comfort, and one's gut is really good at determining what level of risk is appropriate for you," he believes.

Admittedly, fear and logic block us from taking the next step. When I was dating Meredith and marriage became a possibility, I did everything possible to mitigate the risks of what could go wrong. This wasn't a life/death situation, but in many ways, I was acting as if it was. My early childhood experiences set the stage for me to protect my heart at all costs. And that almost cost me the relationship with Meredith. I woke up only after she tossed me out on the street. I crawled back to her, being more vulnerable than I had with any other woman and vowed to do better. Up until then, like many emotionally unavailable men, my fear of intimacy had me circling around a carousel of relationships. I would, at times, connect with one woman, sabotage the relationship, and move on to the next. With Meredith, I knew it was time to surrender to the gift the Universe offered me. My job was to accept it—and that meant risking my heart.

As Michael Singer so aptly stated in *The Surrender Experiment: My Journey Into Life's Perfection*, "Surrender had taught me to willingly participate in life's dance with a quiet mind and an open heart." However, I must admit, this was much harder for me than summiting any mountain.

Alison Levine, author of *On the Edge: Leadership Lessons from Mount Everest and Other Extreme Environments,* says there's a risk of death on many expeditions, whether from being caught in a bad storm or in an avalanche. The key to avoiding being paralyzed by fear is learning to navigate it.

"Fear is just a normal human emotion," says Alison. "If you feel fear, it means you're paying attention to the environment around you. I actually don't see anything wrong with fear."

She believes that most people think of fear as a negative emotion. "I have learned to use fear to my advantage because it keeps me awake, alert, and aware of everything going on around me."

The caveat here is fear is fine as long as it doesn't paralyze you. Doug Holladay says, "If you're risk-averse, you're going to be doing the same thing all the time because you're letting fear dictate how you live your life."

Fears arise from the thoughts we think about day in and day out. Our subconscious is wired to keep us safe, stemming back to the time when stepping out of our caves really could mean life or death. We're on high alert even when we don't need to be, and it's our thoughts—more than 6,200 of them daily, according to the latest research by cognitive neuroscience expert Jordon Poppenk and master's student Julie Tseng from Queens University in Canada—that are running the show.

This means that unless we're very conscious and intentional, we'll be locked into our routines and play small, attempting to ward of any danger—and possibly even death. We'll be stuck in a fixed mindset of "I can't" rather than a growth mindset of "Yes, I can." We stop exploring.

Yet, April Rinne says, "There is nothing like coming face to face with your own mortality to spur you to action. It's for you to make changes, to wake up differently, with a different attitude and perspective. But at the same time, it doesn't 'require' tragedy. The fact is, it is within *everyone's* reach to do this, and I firmly believe that it's a lot easier—and a lot more enjoyable!—to do it *without* the tragedy."

As I mentioned earlier, April experienced a personal tragedy when she was twenty years old when she learned of the tragic death of both of her parents in a car accident. She was in Oxford, England, just hours from leading a summer-long student trip. She describes the following months and years as the equivalent of a midlife crisis, but several decades too soon.

"I started asking the questions back then that, many years later, I see people asking when they're going through some difficult moment or reconciling one's life. But the fact that I was doing so when I was twenty meant that I ended up making very, very different decisions about my career and family and just priorities in general," explains April. "I hadn't come face to face with my own death, but I had been proximate to it. Death had hit me close enough to consider, at a profound level, what I wanted to contribute to the world, what I was capable of, and at the same time, what I was not in control of."

Alison says she likes to put herself in these unpredictable environments. "That's how you learn and grow, and the lessons that you learn in those environments can be applied to almost every other aspect of your life."

Furthermore, as we embark on new endeavors, our level of risk tolerance increases. The more experiences we have, the more we're willing to take risks.

Douglas Holladay believes, "Although this will look different for each of us, I am convinced that we grow and benefit from taking decisive actions that move us beyond the familiar to the frontiers awaiting. A fear-based life is not worth living. The discomfort that comes from venturing into unknown waters brings with it, eventually, after we have gained confidence from the experience, a deep sense of well-being. Only by stretching ourselves can we begin to understand that we are more capable, and that life is less perilous than we might imagine."

Richard Weise recounts the first time he saw people ice climbing near Lake Placid in the Adirondack Mountains. There were people hundreds of feet up there on the sheer walls of ice. And I remember thinking to myself, 'That is absolutely insane. They're going to slip and die,' Years later, I was up there, feeling very comfortable because I knew how the process worked."

Jamie Wheal recounted Transcendentalist philosopher Henry David Thoreau's words: "Most men lead lives of quiet desperation."

To which he adds, "The reality is most people don't have the tolerance capacity or the curiosity to try new things. However, risk tolerance and curiosity bring us alive."

I know that's the elixir of my life.

Reflection

» What brings you joy and happiness?

» What's your level of risk tolerance?

» Where might you be playing small and holding yourself back?

» How might you expand your ability to take risks?

"He who can no longer pause to wonder and stand rapt in awe is as good as dead; his eyes are closed."

— Albert Einstein

CHAPTER 4

SLOWING DOWN
& TUNING IN

In 2005, I was on Everest, and I had nothing else on my mind but summiting. Even with the dangerous effects of the lack of oxygen while closing in on the Death Zone, energy was coursing through my veins. I wanted to hurry up and get to the top. I was amped up. I was gripped. Everything I did, I did fast. There was no time to waste.

And that's when Sherpa Padilla stopped me in my tracks. He told me I packed my backpack too fast. I was taking my tent down too fast. Everything I did was quick. Then he said, "What is making you move so fast?" Essentially, he was concerned that my speed was counterproductive. Instead of being efficient, I was wasting precious energy that I would need to call upon during the climb.

My experience is that many Sherpas, because of their superior adventures on the mountains and cultural roots in Buddhism, focus on being present. In my view, they are wonderful people with big hearts. They consciously connect with each other, with me, and other climbers—and most importantly, with the mountain. And they assist people during the climb (some more than others, of course). I haven't met a climber that doesn't treasure their relationship or relationships with the Sherpas. And their way—and now my way—is to go slow and to conserve energy and oxygen. In my early days of climbing, that barely crossed my mind.

At high altitudes, an ideal goal for some is never to have our heart rate climb above 120 beats per minute. By moving so quickly, I was using too much energy and too much oxygen. That, in effect, jeopardized my possibility of summiting.

The bottom line: I was moving too fast and was operating with what I refer to as an unaware mentality.

What I discovered was that if I just slowed down, I'd enjoy more of my life—both on and off the mountain.

Climb for the Joy

Reflecting upon that climb, where sadly we didn't summit, and a dear friend Rob Milne died on the mountain, I realized at times my life lacked awe, wonder, and presence. I was missing the wonderment in the moment, which means I was missing out on much of my life—-and deep connections with those around me.

Renee Moorefield, CEO of Wisdom Works, says, "Wonder transforms how you perceive the world, no matter who you are or where you live. Approaching situations out of reactivity or fear can cause a tunnel vision that handicaps thinking and decisions while being in a state of positive awe naturally links to greater comfort with uncertainty, creativity, and innovation, an ability to cope with life-work challenges such as isolation and depression, and mental and physical healing."

Thankfully, I've heeded my Sherpa's words and slowed down in many of my pursuits, even when I have the urge to hurry up and get things done. It has allowed me to become more aware of my surroundings, including hazards or opportunities. Additionally, I'm more cognizant of how my energy may affect others and what they might need from me.

April Rinne believes that running slower is a superpower — and one we need to turn to, whether on the mountain or in the boardroom. She stresses that "Going slower also allows you to see when your fellow hikers are struggling, noticing that someone might be dehydrated, noticing that there's a bigger gap between your team than you want there to be. If you're just in your individual pursuit of that mountain, you're going to miss a lot of those things that are about the connectedness of scaling a mountain together — and upon which true success depends."

> "Wonder transforms how you perceive the world, no matter who you are or where you live."
> — Renee Moorefield

Renee Moorefield adds, "A state of wonder is *de-centering*; it is a gateway to transcending your current views about yourself, others, and the complexities you face, even if for a moment. When you're immersed in wonder, you likely feel a healthy self-diminishment — less identified with the ways you usually define yourself and more aware that you are part of something grander — a self-transcending shift that is vital to realizing more of your leadership potential and positive impact."

Kenton Cool and I have had numerous conversations about the joy that arises from that true human connection we find on the mountain — with our fellow climbers, our Sherpas, and the local people whose lives touch ours while we're climbing.

Kenton, who, as I stated earlier, has climbed Everest sixteen times, admits that his first reason for going to Everest is because it's his job. Although, I will argue that as an expedition guide, he hasn't worked a day in his life. But for him, it's more than a paycheck, what he describes as a "deeper, more holistic, and more organic reason" for going back to the mountain. Here's what he recently shared with me:

> "I went to Everest in 2004, but if you rewind the clock to the mid-nineties, I first put together my own expedition while I was doing an undergrad course at the University of Leeds. In my second year, we embarked on an expedition to Pakistan. That was the first time I climbed outside of Europe. And although we didn't set the world on fire with what we were climbing, I was deeply touched and moved by the people of the Himalayas. I was shown generosity and gratitude, unlike anything I'd met before. We climbed a new mountain right at the end of the expedition and dropped off the wrong side of the mountain. We couldn't retreat, nor could we retrace our steps. We'd run out of food, we'd run out of gas, and we couldn't melt the snow into the water. When we finally came off the mountain, these quite desolate, quite scary steep slopes, we entered the high pastures of Pakistan, and we were hit by what I call a smell of life as we came into these green fields.

> "There was a goat herder, a young boy, probably about the same age as us, nineteen. We ended up spending the night with this individual. There were three of us. He invited us into a rudimentary shelter structure. And he shared everything he had with us, which wasn't very much. There was a complete language barrier, but somehow, we overcame that, and there was this deep, deep connection. I simply fell in love with the people of the Himalayas.

> "While a lot has changed on Everest and other mountains in that region, what hasn't changed is the people and the

feeling that most of those lucky enough to be able to go there sense about them.

"You have the Pakistanis, the Afghans, and the Bhutanese people—they are all subtly different yet somehow have this common thread that they live in the mountains," describes Kenton. "They very much are working at a subsistence level. They don't have cars as such until recently. They have no connectivity. It's a very harsh way of life. And I think there is something inherently beautiful about that, something that we have lost in our own society.

"The beauty that's there is the simplicity of living in the moment. These people don't live lightning-fast lives with cell phones constantly ringing, laptops perched within reach, and plane flights jetting us across the nation or around the world. Being in the mountains gives us the opportunity to slow down and tune in to a much higher degree than we possibly could in our day-to-day Western lives.

"When we strip back all the trimmings, noise, or clutter, we realize what true meaning is. I arguably feel more alive when I am in the mountains without the trimmings and without the connectivity."

Tapping into the Unknown

Slowing down also allows us to tap into the energy of the unknown. When we're in the moment, time stands still, and we realize how vast the universe is and how possibility awaits us—if we pause from checking off our to-do list and mindlessly moving through our days, hell-bent on getting to the top of whatever is in front of us. When we're on an expedition, that level of unknown increases mostly because we never know what's going to happen.

"When I'm climbing, I'm wondering slightly where the next meal is going to come from or when it's going to come. I'm not too sure what's going to happen tomorrow. I'm not sure where my journey will take me," explains Kenton. "That elevates my attunement to my surroundings, and suddenly, I become hyperfocused. I become hypersensitized to life. When you walk the tightrope between light and dark. And I don't mean day and night. I mean life and death, and you peer into the abyss, genuinely believing that you potentially are not going to come back—there is total clarity on what we actually have."

Yet, we don't always need to stare death in the face, but we can do things outside our comfort zone to push ourselves. "We won't always know what those things might be until we've slowed down enough to hear the soul's calling," says Kenton. "It could be running a 10K, it could be rock climbing, or it simply could be taking a walk in the park with an old friend and really listening to what they're saying."

One could argue that those of us who embrace extreme adventures invite awe into our lives. Not only are we faced with our mortality, but in those moments clinging to the side of the mountain, we can, as I experienced when I was a young boy, be cocooned in a state that enhances our well-being on multiple levels. Each of these moments primes the pump to seek out other adventures to keep us more closely attuned to the wonder in our lives.

Beau Lotto, who is a professor of neuroscience at University College London and CEO of a neuroscience research group called the Lab of Misfits, discovered that our brains and our behaviors change as a result of encountering moments that have evoked awe. Respondents to Lotto's survey stated that they were more willing to take risks and become more comfortable with uncertainty. Additionally, they redefined their perceptions of themselves.

Kenton adds, "That goat herder arguably is the lucky one, and that's coming from a person of a privileged background, and if I don't like that way of life, I can step out of it. I realize that that guy back in Pakistan has no choice. So, it's easy for me to say he's the lucky one. But honestly, look at all the misery in our world—depression, the opiate crisis, the addiction issues, the crime elevated in our society—compared with mountain societies. Why is that? That's the question we got to ask ourselves. And my belief is because we have become too comfortable. We have too many trappings. We've lost sight of what is actually important to us, as human beings, as a community. And as a society, we've lost that tribal collectiveness which you still have in the mountains where there is hardship, deprivation, and uncertainty."

> "We've lost that tribal collectiveness which you still have in the mountains where there is hardship, deprivation, and uncertainty."
>
> —Kenton Cool

In their article, "Awe, the Small Self, and Prosocial Behavior," researchers Paul Piff and his colleagues found, "Awe, although often fleeting and hard to describe, serves a vital social function. By diminishing the emphasis on the individual self, awe may encourage people to forego strict self-interest to improve the welfare of others."

It's likely that the goat herder is in a continual state of awe surrounded by the majestic peaks of the Himalayas, as are those who honor their symbiotic relationship with nature. But we don't always have to leave our families and trek off to some distant mountain to step into wonder.

In her article, "Healing Trauma with Awe and Wonder," Gina Simmons Schneider, PhD shared that awe can be evoked right in our backyards and very simply. One suggestion she makes is a

"Sensing walk: Take a slow walk in a park, canyon, or near a lake, ocean, or another place of natural diversity. Put away your phone and pay attention to what your body senses. Notice the sound of crunching leaves under your feet—bird song, the wind through the trees, the lapping of water. Notice the temperature and how light plays on the landscape. Slowly examine the trees, shrubs, flowers, insects, and any other life you see. Notice the texture and colors of a rock, the sand, clay soil, or the feel of a leaf or pinecone. Smell the bark of a tree, a leaf, a flower, the air. Let yourself notice each sensation as if for the first time."

I firmly believe that getting outside every day is important for our bodies, minds, and souls. And there's nothing like sharing a stroll to the park, a walk around a lake, or a hike up a mountain with family or friends.

And with a sense of community firmly rooted in our lives, we can withstand everything, even in the darkest times of the unknown. We'll explore more of this in Chapter 9.

The Power of Intuition

Slowing down also nurtures our intuition. That hyperfocused and hypersensitivity that Kenton mentioned is crucial both on and off the mountain. While to many, it seems that I do run too fast, and admittedly there are times that I do, I have a daily practice of gratitude. Each day, I write down all that I'm grateful for in my life. This shifts my mindset from focusing on what might not be working to all that is. Often the balance of what is working far outweighs the deficit of what isn't. When I'm in a positive frame of mind, I'm able to tap more readily into my intuition—knowing instinctively what moves to make both on and off the mountain.

Most highly successful people advocate building contemplation and creative time into their calendars. That's where our innovative ideas can bubble to the surface and capture our attention.

That's how our intuition makes its way through all the noise of our lives. It's not a passive act to slow down. It takes an act of commitment—and sometimes courage—to be willing to see what might arise during these quieter times of our day.

April Rinne, who says she learned to nurture her sixth sense, says, "When I say run slower, I'm not saying stop. I'm not saying be lazy. I'm saying slow down to make sure that you can actually see what's really happening. That can be on a mountain or in life."

While she was raised in a family that believed in therapy and journaling about her feelings, she wasn't noticing the subtle clues that our intuition often gives us. Notably, some signs are "overt," such as a closed trail or a promotion we didn't get. Yet, much of what is conveyed through our intuition is invisible.

Understanding one's intuition takes work and practice. It's not always an immediate gut reaction followed by an action. She describes her process as one where she gets a sense that there's something going on that can't be seen.

Paying Attention to the Unseen

As a kid, I wasn't aware of the subtle messages around me, but the more I climbed, the more I paid attention to the signs that alerted me to potential danger. I even learned to ask for signs from God, which often came to me from nature.

For instance, I wanted to be the first American to summit Manaslu, meaning the spirit of the mountain and the eighth-highest mountain in the Nepalese Himalayas. I was climbing really fast, even questioning myself if my pace was too quick. Then, I became aware of one high-altitude bird who seemed to be following me. I watched this bird soaring near me, all the while questioning whether my pursuit of summiting the mountain was right.

So, I said to myself, "Well, it's very simple. I've seen this bird for the last six hours by itself. If there's another bird with that bird, then that other bird would be Meredith. And that means I have to go back because I have a family." The moment I said that, within thirty seconds boom, another bird appeared. They were flying side by side. I'd gotten my sign—I turned around.

My curiosity, paired with a sense that something was not quite right on this climb, led me to one of the wisest decisions of my life. If I hadn't questioned if I was going too fast, if I hadn't slowed down enough to become aware of my surroundings, I might have missed those birds—and I might not be writing this book today.

Robert Moss, a pioneer of Active Dreaming, an original synthesis of shamanism and modern dreamwork, says, "The world is full of signs and symbols and will give us a bit of a dreamlike story if we pay attention, and that can be very exciting, very empowering."

My guess is that paying attention to that bird and then testing the Universe with my dare that if two birds appeared that represented Meredith and myself meant I needed to go back, I might have averted disaster. Over the years of mountaineering, my innate sense of knowing when to turn around has become more refined. My "dare" was simply a way to test it. The appearance of the birds wasn't just a matter of luck—but a way that I've come to communicate with a higher power.

In fact, Moss says, "If you're open to the idea that the world might be speaking to you, you can get a useful message. If you play the game and you're open to what the world gives you, you'll begin to discover these things for yourself."

For April Rinne, curiosity quells the fear of the unknown and overrides our tendency to rely only upon what is comfortable and familiar. She says it's a universal phenomenon that humans typically see what we've been trained by our families and culture to see. "Every culture or every person is faced with this reality. But as a result, not a single person sees the full picture. The best anyone can do is become aware of, and then learn to see, what they are missing."

April also believes when one is fully present and possesses a high level of self-awareness, it's easier to sense when something is off, or someone is struggling. Genuine connection with people on our teams is also key to using the power of inquiry to see what might be lurking beneath the surface. "Your job as a leader is to help people express what they're holding back so that you can have the conversation that brings you together again," she adds.

> "Curiosity quells the fear of the unknown and overrides our tendency to rely only upon what is comfortable and familiar."
>
> — April Rinne

In other words, we have to slow down and peer into the invisible. Without doing that, we actually may be hurting our chances of survival, whether we're climbing an actual mountain or one in our career or relationships, especially when a crisis arises.

Tools for Tuning In

Olympic Gold Medalist Kathy Kreiner-Phillips, who now has a consulting business for individuals to develop a stronger mindset for better success in sports and life, says, "Meditation practice is one of the best tools for athletes to be their best, as well to create that space where they're able to focus on what's in their control and blocking out what they can't control." She affirms that slowing down and committing to her meditation practice has been key to staying in touch with herself—and to her success, particularly in the '76 Olympics.

"I took a little break before the '76 Olympics to visit a friend because I wasn't having the results I wanted, and I didn't feel prepared to win at this point," Kathy says.

Her friend, a philosophy student, not an athlete, encouraged her to identify how she wanted to feel pushing out of the starting gate. During her meditations, she began visualizing her run down the slope.

"I did a little meditation, and I would visualize looking ahead, being on my outside ski, and feeling centered," she says. "It was the most relaxed I've ever felt, and I never got distracted, even with spectators shouting 'Rosi,' for German Rosi Mittermeier, who had already won two golds and was expected to win everything. I simply saw those people as trees."

Pro-skateboarder Mitchie Brusco takes a similar approach to his skateboarding run. Mitchie, who turned pro at age fourteen, says he spends about as much time visualizing his runs as actually practicing them. And it's paid off. The Encinitas, California, resident has won numerous X Games championships.

Elizabeth Gould advocates engaging the emotions to feel what it is we want to experience at some point in the future, which she refers to in the *Feeling Forwards* process.

But to do this, we have to slow down. We have to understand what it is we want, be willing to listen to the cues the Universe sends to us—and know we deserve the success we desire—just because we are who we are. Tuning into those whispers of our soul makes all the difference in the world.

"When we learn to run slower, the outcomes are better across the board: wiser decisions, less stress, greater resilience, improved health, a stronger connection with our emotions and intuition, presence, focus, and clarity of purpose," says April Rinne. "Paradoxically, slowing down gives us more time, leading to less anxiety. Slowing down enhances our productivity in ways that matter and sends burnout to the dustbin. In reality, there are many kinds of growth that can come only with rest—including the ability to see the amazing you that you've always been."

Richard Wiese, who has spent his life exploring and learning about countries and cultures, once shared a story about a man who boasted of visiting 190 countries in 20 months, and the only one he hadn't set foot upon was North Korea. "I thought to myself, *'How pathetic,'* I thought to myself, *'How pathetic. What did he really experience or learn?'*" Richard adds, "We've become a society of people looking to check things off a list. I'm seeing a dangerous trend in national parks where people are going to where it says the best photo spot. Then they take the picture and feel like, 'Okay, I've done it.' There are so many wonderful things that happen on the trails, in self-discovery or with companions, that aren't marked by a selfie location."

Doug Holladay, founder, and director of PathNorth, an organization that promotes discussions of meaning and purpose among leaders and executives, believes that instead of running faster, we all need to run slower to be able to acknowledge where life might not be working for us. In particular, he believes many of us define our success extrinsically.

"If you're a human, you must keep doing it to be validated. If you're a human being, that is a very, very different way you think about yourself, and there isn't a lot of help for that journey. You've got to figure it out yourself," Doug explains.

And to do that, we need to slow down and tune in. In 1666, Blaise Pascal, the physicist, inventor, and philosopher, said, "All of humanity's problems stem from man's inability to quietly sit alone in a room."

Doug believes that if we could learn to be alone, what would show up for most achievers could be the answer to what they are truly seeking—success defined by our soul's calling.

Ultimately, if we're running too fast and we're distractible, we're missing out on a lot of life—our own. And while I could probably slow down another notch or two at times, I've learned to appreciate allowing myself a quiet time of reflection and even the simple pleasures of shooting hoops with my boys or playing video games.

The Nature Connection

Nature provides us with the best way to slow down and disconnect from our devices, to-do lists, and anything else that disrupts our peace. As I've shared earlier, climbing mountains is like meditation. And whenever I'm home, my family and I make a habit of taking Saturday morning hikes together.

Richard Louv, who has written many books on the restorative power of nature, including *The Nature Principle: Human Restoration and the End of the Nature-Deficit Disorder*, says, "The future will belong to the nature-smart — those individuals, families, businesses, and political leaders who develop a deeper understanding of the transformative power of the natural world and who balance the virtual with the real. The more high-tech we become, the more nature we need."

Through his extensive research, Louv has discovered "how tapping into the restorative powers of the natural world can boost mental acuity and creativity; promote health and wellness; build smarter and more sustainable businesses, communities, and economies; and ultimately strengthen human bonds."

So, think of ways that you might tap into the power of nature to slow down and connect with yourself and with family, friends, and colleagues. Take your meetings outside. Instead of meeting for coffee, go for a walk. Give yourself space, as my friend Kenton Cool says, "to let your mind wander into different atmospheres that normally it doesn't" within the confines of your homes and offices.

Reflection

» Where in life have you been running too fast?

» How might you give yourself permission to
slow down?

» What would be the first act toward doing that?

» How would your leadership—in business, with your
family, or in your community—benefit from slowing
down and tuning into your intuition?

"You gotta act. You gotta be willing to fail. You gotta be willing to crash and burn...if you're afraid you'll fail, you won't get very far."

— Steve Jobs, Founder of Apple

CHAPTER 5

FALLING IS NOT FAILING

O n any mountain there's always the chance of falling, and I've had more than one of those. One particular incident comes to mind: Aoraki Mount Cook in New Zealand. The area is known for its rugged peaks, verdant alpine valleys, and spectacular glaciers. My guide and I were climbing the Linda Glacier route, which started in the dark. The day became epic. Bright sunshine, bluebird skies, and breathtaking views filled me with a sense of peace and gratitude.

Several hours had passed, and I was in the moment, enjoying each step with the crunch of ice beneath my feet. While the weather was still in our favor, because of the altitude, the air temperatures had fallen. I was focused on my breath, carefully assessing each of my steps, and very present. The rush of time had ceased, and I was in a meditative state, one that I often access on my climbs — now that I've learned to slow down.

Glaciers hold their own challenges, and one of them is that at any moment, there might be a hole in the ice (or snow bridge), one that is either visible or one we accidentally find with a wrong step.

Suddenly, I felt a tug on my rope. Instantly, I knew my guide had fallen and was in a terrible spot. Moments later, I was face down on the ice and sliding with increasing speed toward a hole in the ice. As I slipped over the edge, I was convinced I was doomed, and then the rope went taught, and I jerked to an abrupt stop. My guide had successfully self-arrested by jamming his icepick into a solid section of the glacier—and not a moment too soon. I was dangling over a crevasse, hundreds of feet from the ground below.

Ordinarily, one would think that moving quickly would be called for, but through my training I understood that remaining calm and deliberate in my actions would prevent me from plunging to my death.

With the temperatures even colder with ice all around me, I put on my jacket, and then donned a heavier pair of gloves. Slowly, with my guide holding steady above me, I climbed out of that hole. I'd brushed along death's door once again and walked away.

Choosing Perseverance

While there have been numerous times when I've fallen on the mountain, in business, and with my relationships, it was as a young boy where the idea that I was a failure was first planted and became an almost impossible obstacle to overcome. Dyslexia and ADHD were formidable obstacles not only to my success in school, but also greatly diminished my self-esteem and self-worth. I'd all but committed to a life of being a royal screw up, doing nothing right and making no one happy with me.

Fortunately, my parents hired a tutor, Gail Allman. One day, frustrated beyond belief that I just couldn't comprehend the simplest text staring at me from the pages of a book, I said to her, "I just keep failing."

She said, "Bo, I've never I've never seen you fail."

"Well, what do you mean?" I was curious. How could she not see how I rarely got anything right!

"Because you've never given up."

Her response stays with me to this day and rests in my heart as a reminder that I never give up, even when I might be on my knees in what appears to be the ultimate defeat. Somehow, something inside me — often combined with the support of those around me — ushers in the courage to begin again.

Experience has taught me that failure is inevitable. It's how we learn. Unfortunately, our families, our schools, and our businesses — our culture in general — discount the value of failing. Instead, we're taught to strive for perfection, which in itself is impossible. Perfection is a moving target in a world that is ever-changing and unpredictable. It's usually based on other people's moods, whims, and their own ideas of how we fit into their stories.

With that mindset, we're not taught to prepare for failure. Preparing to fall is what has saved me, not only on Mt. Cook and other expeditions, but in life as well.

Failing is also where we grow. In those moments of failure, we gain the wisdom, character, and understanding that allow us to move to the next level of our life adventures.

Like, Nims Purja says, "If you don't give up, you won't die." Purja is a renowned mountaineer whose spectacular feat of climbing all 14 eight-thousanders (mountain peaks above 8,000 meters or 26,000 feet) in six months and six days with oxygen is evidence of his belief that if we keep on striving, we'll never fail.

> "If you don't give up, you won't die."
> — Nims Purja

My Biggest Test

However, there were times in my life when adversity cast a shadow upon my life that I not only felt like I was failing, I thought I was dying—or wished I was.

A former company, Jumar Management, which I co-founded with a partner, made investments in distressed consumer debt and other asset classes. Years into the business, we were alerted by federal regulators that one of the companies we allocated capital to was involved in what turned out to be a highly complex fraud. In essence, we and many others fell for a Ponzi scheme, and as a result, the Jumar Investors, including many friends and family members, lost money.

It's hard, even now, years later, to describe the widespread impact on so many people I care about and my feelings of despair over what happened. For months after receiving the call that the FBI had been doing a lengthy undercover investigation and had raided that business, I was incapable of showing up for myself, my wife, and my children. I did show up daily for the investors and took their calls, as this brought me energy. It was the worst feeling I've ever had in my life. Devastated doesn't even touch the gravity of my emotional state. I was always throwing up, even when nothing would come out because I hadn't eaten. I just died. I was alive, but I was dead inside.

My health suffered. My marriage suffered, and I didn't have the energy to be the dad my sons deserved. Night after night, I lay in my bed, in a fetal position, in the darkest space I'd ever experienced. I didn't see a way out. That time period lasted quite some time and was harder than climbing Mt. Everest.

Somehow, God's grace sought me out, even though I didn't feel like I deserved one iota. A couple of our investors, Marc Butler and his partner Matt Calkins planted a seed that began changing my perspective. Their company is a glass and fenestration expert located in Colorado, and they've seen their share of ups and downs.

During one of my darker periods, Marc said to me: "Bo, do you think I didn't know the risk? I didn't have to do anything, and you were making me 30%. Do you think I didn't know that when I invested that this might be a complete write-off?"

Then Marc shared how they operate their business on the Toyota Production System. Focusing particularly on the problem-solving cycle, he explains, "The problem-solving cycle looks like this. You make a plan around a problem, right? And normally, what happens in the Plan–Do–Check–Act cycle. You make a plan. You do the plan. Then you check back in. Generally, when faced with a complete failure, it's time to pick yourself up, dust yourself off, and make another plan based on what you just learned. You execute that plan, and you check back in. This is why humility is a core attribute for us. We must be able to accept failure and then step back and assess what needs to happen to get on our feet again."

Matt, who is an engineer, added another important perspective. "Step seven of the production cycle is reflection, especially on the process that attains the results. What I saw from Bo's project were bad results and good process," he shares. "I truly believe what he was doing was smart, and he could have done it again and made it work all day long."

I spent a great deal of time reflecting upon their wisdom. It didn't sink in entirely right away, but one of Matt's comments played over and over in my mind. "Growth necessarily requires problems." This problem was a bitter pill to swallow, making all those on the mountains seem pale in comparison.

Another glimmer of hope followed shortly thereafter through the words of my friend, Nate Klemp. He said, "Sometimes, you can find a little break by prayer."

So, I started praying more, and at first, I felt nothing. And I kept praying hundreds of times a day. I prayed for our investors. I prayed that the incredible pain that had paralyzed me would go away. I prayed to show up and be a dad to my kids.

And slowly, with God's grace, I began to emerge from that dark hole.

I discovered that during our darkest times, we come to know who our friends are. Nate, Marc, and Matt were not the only ones. I received numerous calls from friends and family telling me to hang in there, saying it wasn't my fault. That we'd been blindsided.

Emotionally, spiritually, mentally, and physically, I abandoned myself and all those closest to me whom I love, particularly my kids. And while it may seem counterintuitive, I knew I couldn't show up for them as their dad until I figured out what happened and found some way to make things right.

One way to do that was to testify in front of the grand jury against the company that had scammed us and many others. And still, it was hard for me to be there for my sons. I was embarrassed.

Then one day, another intervention knocked at my consciousness. I was walking down Pearl Street in Boulder, and Bob Litwin, who wrote the book, *Live the Best Story of Your Life: A World Champion's Guide to Lasting Change,* and a performance coach for athletes and executives, saw me. He said, "Hey, I love that you're fighting for your investors. That's great. And I'm very concerned about you. You're not keeping your health and not connecting with your family. You should never let those go." That was another shift.

> "Failure is the opportunity to begin again more intelligently."
> — Henry Ford

What I've discovered is that in the duality of life, it's not all sunshine and rainbows all the time. The dark is needed to show us the light. Everyone has their own pain and suffering. And ultimately, these difficult situations don't define who we are when we're brave enough to look inside and see our own goodness.

The circumstances with Jumar dished up a hard lesson, but I've learned a great deal about how to come back even stronger (which isn't easy by any measure).

Become the Apprentice

By coming out the other side of that experience, I've had to face the fear of failing over and over. In some ways, the Jumar debacle was a kind of apprenticeship where life became my biggest teacher.

Richard Wiese says apprenticeship is where we gather the building blocks to success. He also believes those building blocks are key to creating a greater awareness that might avert danger.

"When you hear certain athletes talking about things happening in slow motion, it's because they have a wealth of experience and that they're able to see certain signs way before they even happen," explains Richard. "It's that cumulative knowledge that allows us to have a greater vision of what's around us — and continue to evolve and learn."

Dreamwork expert Robert Moss says, "If you're open to the idea that the world might be speaking to you, you can get useful messages. You can receive a little bit of magic for the day, then you'll notice more on your road."

Alex Weber says that brave honesty with ourselves is vital to watch for ways we might sabotage ourselves and overlook warning signs that could lead to failure.

"We live in a time where there are so many distractions, there's so much noise, there are so many escapisms, that it can be really easy to not look at the tough stuff," he explains. "Sometimes, if I get an email or a call, my impulse will be to grab my phone, and I stop myself and ask: What is it that I don't want to deal with?"

To attain clarity amidst all of the noise, turning to what Robert Moss refers to as Sidewalk Tarot could provide the insights we need to overcome our troubles—or find a positive direction in our lives.

While competing on *American Ninja Warrior,* Alex learned what it was like to fail tangibly. But the more subtle failures in life often are classes that we don't pass, arguments with loved ones, or even missing a turn on the highway. "We first have an emotional reaction," he says. "We're pissed off or angry. We're frustrated. And then we disengage."

That's where we miss the opportunity that failure offers us. Alex calls this the golden nugget—a time when we can examine how we might not have prepared or could have shown up with more presence with a client or loved one with whom we're now in disagreement.

"Our emotions serve us," he explains. "We don't necessarily need to go to peaks and valleys, but we do need to question our limiting beliefs. For instance, one of my limiting beliefs is that I don't want to bother people. I had to realize that it's up to them to decide if I'm a bother or a blessing. My job is in showing up and doing the things that need to be done."

Alex says that during times of setbacks we get to recommit. "It's not glamorous and exponential, but if you take time to re-examine a failure, you will reach your goal, your relationships will improve, your career will improve, and your personal life will improve."

Rick Hanson, PhD, author of *Just One Thing: Developing a Buddha Brain One Simple Practice,* and Senior Fellow of UC Berkeley's Greater Good Science Center, says we can rely on our innate intuition to guide us through life—the good times and the challenging ones. The problem is that our inner intelligence is overshadowed by our cultural conditioning, including family systems and the media. Yet, it doesn't have to be, as evidenced by Nikola Tesla, Albert Einstein, Richard Branson, and Steve Jobs.

Rick explains, "Most of our top entrepreneurs and leaders have made room for and listen to their deeper inner guidance. These leaders were more willing to make time for their intuitive intelligence. They go slower and ask questions. They tune in and create space for that in their decision making."

This, he adds, separates them from the rest of the pack. "They literally have an invisible edge over their competition because they have the courage to really listen deeply and follow that intelligence and a higher level of innovation. That's inside all of us, but they had the courage to listen to it and take action on it, which really separated them from others."

While it took me far longer than I'd hoped, I did engage in brave honesty with myself. I slowed down. I tuned in and now more readily trust my inner guidance. I recommitted to my health, my marriage, and my boys. And I reminded myself of my long-term goals, knowing that failure might always be lurking around any corner—but I could bounce back from it. To do that, I had to rebuild my resilience. Luckily, my difficult childhood set the stage for me to build a healthy reservoir of resilience. Plus, over the years, I've discovered how to refill that reservoir when life challenges drained me to my core.

There are a number of ways to increase our resilience, and self-care is one of them. Driving ourselves into the ground never helps anyone. I've come to that understanding the hard way on multiple occasions. My self-care obviously includes getting out in nature, reflecting on what's going right in my world in my gratitude journal, and getting enough sleep to sustain my level of activity. Sleep is crucial.

"Today, much of our society is still operating under the collective delusion that sleep is simply time lost to other pursuits, that it can be endlessly appropriated at will to satisfy our increasingly busy lives and overstuffed to-do lists," writes Ariana Huffington in her book,

The Sleep Revolution: Transforming Your Life, One Night at a Time.
"The combination of a deeply misguided definition of what it means
to be successful in today's world—that it can come only through
burnout and stress—along with the distractions and temptations of
a 24/7 wired world, has imperiled our sleep as never before."

I've also adopted several self-talk practices that assist me in
times when I must override that negative self-doubt that has
followed me like a dark cloud many moments in my life. In
addition to affirmations where I use "I am" to begin my statements,
such as "I am an amazing dad," I've discovered that saying, "You,
Bo, are an amazing dad," is more effective.

Steve Magness, a mental performance coach and author of
*Do Hard Things: Why We Get Resilience Wrong and the Surprising
Science of Real Toughness*, says switching from "I" to "You" or
"We" in our self-talk establishes "distance between an experience
and our emotional response."

Essentially, what he's discovered is that the use of "I" creates
"a self-immersed perspective [which] amplifies the emotional
aspects of the situation. Our world narrows and we get drawn into
the emotionality of the experience, setting ourselves up for the
negative cascade toward choosing the 'easy path' in our toughness
paradigm."

Additionally, he adds, "When we create psychological
distance, our view of the world broadens. We can let go of the
emotionality—seeing the world clearly for what it is, instead of
letting it spiral."

Reframing Failure

Marcus Baur, Olympic Yacht racer and creator of Goalscape, says,
"Failure is the normal state of affairs. A lot of people who don't
have long-term goals think if I fail, that's it. Those who have long-
term goals don't care about failure. They just get back up. You got

to have a long-term vision and believe in yourself, and then you've got to be ready to fail and to fall down. But you'll also need to pace your way to your goal in a way where you have intermediate successes."

Marcus explained that when training for the Olympics, he was always digging for what others referred to as mistakes. "For me, they were not mistakes. They were opportunities, and I was encouraging people to tell me where I messed up," he adds. "I wanted to know because that's where I could potentially improve."

> "Failure is the normal state of affairs. A lot of people who don't have long-term goals think if I fail, that's it. Those who have long-term goals don't care about failure. They just get back up."
>
> — Marcus Baur

Seeing an opportunity to grow reframes the whole concept of failure.

Marcus also believes that social safety nets need to be in place when people fail—not to rest on, but to find new inspiration and to do new great things. Mark Butler, Matt Calkins, and Nate Klemp were essentially my safety net.

Jason Valadao, MD, author of *Exceptional Every Day,* says, "Our subconscious drives so much of what we do, and that's what derails us. We set this goal, and when someone tells us something, or we see something on social media that makes us question our goal or ability, we totally get offset."

The idea then is to keep our eye on the goal and to be ever mindful of anything that might trip us up. I'm always watchful for the little voice inside of me that tells me that I'm never good enough or that I always fail. During past experiences, that voice became louder, and I had to work hard to put it in its place. And I know I'm not alone. Many high achievers face the same inner critic at periods in their lives.

Alex Weber explained that he built up this internal false belief that he always failed. He was able to turn that belief around by realizing there was another possibility. In 2020, he missed the *American Ninja Warrior* season with a broken thumb. His waistline was expanding, and he didn't think he'd ever get back into shape well enough to compete. "There comes a point where you need to start to communicate to yourself that this other possibility could exist even though you don't see it." Once one acknowledges the possibility, the next step is to take action, something he refers to as the Action-Belief Cycle in his book, *Fail Proof: Become the Unstoppable.*

That action, whether it's difficult or messy, forms the foundation for a new possibility and the fuel for you to show up again and again. "I've seen *American Ninja,* where we film ourselves and look at our form. And there's been times I'll watch my videos and think, 'Oh, my gosh, I look like a sack of potatoes.' And then there are other times when I'm thinking, 'That's actually pretty good like that. That looks like an athlete doing it.' Then this new foundational belief summons bigger actions. So, I would say step one is simply believe in possibility," he says.

> "The beautiful truth is that anything in this entire world is learnable — if you're willing to give your best, manage your emotions, mine for your golden nugget, and then keep going."
> — Alex Weber

"The beautiful truth is that anything in this entire world is learnable — if you're willing to give your best, manage your emotions, mine for your golden nugget, and then keep going," adds Alex.

I've had to mine for my golden nugget in relationship failures and in business. I now view what I once perceived as failures as course corrections, often guiding me to better places in my life. Without the failed relationships with the women I dated, I wouldn't have met Meredith and had two amazing sons. Had Jumar continued, I wouldn't now be in my role at DLP Capital, where I feel like I am having a daily positive impact on people's lives. To get to that place, I had to tap into my inner wisdom, acknowledge the problem, and figure out ways to solve it.

Others have done the same. Kathy Kreiner-Phillips fell into a funk after her 1976 Olympic Gold win and went through a period of time when she wasn't performing well on the slopes. "When I won, that was my soul voice speaking loudly to me. It was such a strong sense of knowing I would win. It was very intuitive. I could relax and let it happen," she says.

Unfortunately, that win was followed by several failures at the World Cup circuit. Her post-win mindset wished she was just sitting in a cafe having a coffee. "I threw away these two races because I just wasn't up for it mentally."

In part, she was battling her own inner disappointment but also facing the disappointment of others. She became so intrigued by the concept of how others' expectations impact our behaviors and our decisions that she went on to do her master's research on how to continue to be successful once we've had success. "It's the challenge to deal with those expectations—yours and those that others put on you—and to do it repeatedly."

Stress and burnout are often contributing factors to success, as Kathy discovered. She said many people didn't know how to deal with her success, and when she wasn't succeeding, it added even more pressure to her already challenged mindset.

"I was so down in the dumps and believed I should just quit," she explains. "But I had this mind shift between runs. Our Northern Ontario Ski Team happened to be there training. They all wanted to meet me. So I had to snap out of my funk and be the athlete."

Kathy said she began watching the first racers in the competition do their runs and noticed something she hadn't previously—their level of aggression. "They were like wild animals going after their prey. I thought, 'I'm just going to take on that level of aggression and give it all I have,' And I won the second run." That mindset shift gave Kathy the confidence to keep going.

Essentially, she had to pull up her bootstraps and recommit in Alex Weber's terms. In doing so, she became aligned with her soul calling—that sense she possessed when winning the gold.

We often need to get into action to overcome our sense of failure. If we stay paralyzed, nothing ever changes.

Ryan Holiday, author of *The Obstacle is the Way: The Timeless Art of Turning Trials into Triumph*, writes, "There have been countless lessons (and books) about achieving success, but no one ever taught us how to overcome failure, how to think about obstacles, how to treat and triumph over them, so we are stuck. Beset on all sides, many of us are disoriented, reactive, and torn. We have no idea what to do."

When Jumar collapsed, I truly didn't know what to do. I'd come from a long line of successful businessmen, and here I failed miserably. In addition to the encouragement from my friends, I turned to those who walked before me for inspiration.

One of the great orators in history is Demosthenes, who suffered a speech impediment like me. From him, I've gleaned the importance of having what Holiday describes as "a relentless drive to improve himself through action and practice." While Demosthenes was born to a wealthy family, when orphaned, he was stripped of his inheritance by his guardians and essentially left "for dead." But he refused to be beaten down. He locked himself away to "fill his mouth with pebbles and practice speaking," explains Ryan. "And soon, his quiet, weak voice erupted with a booming, powerful clarity."

That clarity is what gave him the confidence to file a lawsuit against his guardians, which he eventually won. "Only a fraction of the original inheritance remained, but the money had become secondary," writes Ryan. "Demosthenes's reputation as an orator, ability to command a crowd, and his peerless knowledge of the intricacies of the law, was worth more than whatever remained of a once-great fortune."

Demosthenes took action. He used his obstacle as a way to claim victory and pursue his dreams. Teddy Roosevelt would say that he stepped into the arena of life. He said:

> It is not the critic who counts; not the man who points out how the strong man stumbles, or where the doer of deeds could have done them better. The credit belongs to the man who is actually in the arena, whose face is marred by dust and sweat and blood; who strives valiantly; who errs, who comes short again and again, because there is no effort without error and shortcoming; but who does actually strive to do the deeds; who knows great enthusiasms, the great devotions; who spends himself in a worthy cause; who at the best knows, in the end, the triumph of high achievement, and who at the worst, if he fails, at least fails while daring greatly, so that his place shall never be with those cold and timid souls who neither know victory nor defeat.

Alison Levine says, "Failure is just one thing that happens to you at one point in time. If you're so afraid to fail, then you're going to be risk-averse. And, in order for innovation to happen at a rapid pace, you have to really have a sense of failure tolerance in the corporate world."

For a time, I did allow my failure to define me. But I rallied. I remembered, in Elizabeth Gould's terms, my aim. I picked up the pieces of my life and recommitted to the bigger vision to have a positive impact on the world, whether I was climbing a mountain and raising money for charity or improving people's lives through my business ventures.

As Doug Holladay reminds us, "To do great things, we need to be able to endure tragedy and setbacks. We've got to be able to love what we do and all that it entails, good and bad. We have to learn to find joy in every single thing that happens."

And I have.

Reflection

» When have you experienced failure and how did you view it?

» If failure brought you to your knees, how did you find the strength to rise again?

» What do you believe lead to your failure?

» What support system do you have around you for when those obstacles appear on your path?

"Things don't go wrong and break your heart, so you can become bitter and give up. They happen to break you down and build you up so you can be all that you were intended to be."

— *Charlie Tremendous Jones,*
author of Life Is Tremendous:
Enthusiasm Makes a Difference

CHAPTER 6

BREAKING DOWN & REBUILDING

B reaking down frequently happens on expeditions, especially when expectations are not set and contingency plans are made for those inevitable disruptions in the perfectly made plan. My climb on Denali was no exception. I hired a guide company to coordinate my climb, and I was assigned to three rope teams, with one guide assigned to each team of three climbing members. I happen to be climbing with a friend of mine. Unfortunately, before the climb even began, he hurt his ankle and slowed down our team quite a bit. I trained my body to climb quickly, and after two days, I was tired. I wasn't prepared to carry an 80-pound pack and 80-pound sled for an extra four or five hours each day.

Seeking a solution to my pain and suffering—and my friend's, knowing he felt guilty for slowing me down—I asked to be placed on one of the faster teams but was denied. I saw this as a win-win for everyone. My friend had the opportunity to work one-to-one with a guide, and I would be able to pick up my pace. The lead guide didn't see the wisdom in this, and so for another three or four days, I toiled up the mountain at a grueling slow pace. I knew I could not continue for another two weeks. I was done.

My body was breaking down, my mood was deteriorating, and I was beginning to resent the guide team and my friend. So, I confronted the lead guide one more time, and a shouting match ensued. Things definitely went from bad to worse.

Fortunately, after both of us cooled our heels, he saw the wisdom in my suggestion, and the teams were restructured. I joined a faster team, and my friend was able to get the individual attention he needed.

What I learned is that oftentimes relationships need to be broken down and rebuilt, and when that occurs, quite often, it's in everyone's best interest.

Breaking Down My Relationship with My Father

My relationship with my father had been difficult at times throughout my life. I never had the connection with him that I desired. He had his other family and worked long hours, so I rarely saw him. However, on an emotional and spiritual level, I kept him on a pedestal. And I was constantly trying to get him to see me and value me.

Despite our challenges, I also worked for my father for a couple of years in his healthcare company, MPI Research. In the two years, I increased the revenue of my division by more than 40% in each of those years—even during the second worst economic downturn in modern history (2009 and 2010), but it was obvious that my dad never planned to turn the business over to me (or anyone for that matter). This was his baby, and so I chose to move on to the next opportunity, which for a time added to the tension between us.

My dad and I had to break down our relationship to have any chance at a loving father-son bond. First, I had to see him with all his imperfections, and I had to accept myself as I am, owning my own strengths and weaknesses. Without that, I would never have stopped seeking his approval.

When we redefined our relationship, we focused on our personal relationship and left the business on the table. That chapter of our lives had passed. We determined that it was far more important for our father/son relationship to thrive--and for him to be a wonderful grandfather to my sons.

Today, he and I have frequent visits and phone conversations. He also gets to be a grandpa to my sons, which brings much joy to all of us. We have a great relationship.

Breaking Down My Marriage

Before Meredith and I got married, I tried to solve all sorts of contingencies with a prenuptial agreement on even the tiniest of matters. Finally, one of my mentors said, "Bo, it's marriage, and it requires an absolute leap of faith. You're never going to know. You just have to make your best effort."

During parts of our marriage, I wasn't making my best effort. I was selfishly focused on my own agendas—mountain climbing and building my business, Iconic Development, which developed student housing real estate projects. I ignored numerous signs that my marriage could have been improved. Signs that grew more urgent as time passed. First, there were the Tap-Taps, where Meredith gently asked, "Do you have to train today? Can't you spend it with your family? Or could we have a date night this week?"

And then there were the Knock-Knocks when Meredith was visibly upset with me. One time she said, "Bo, I'm upset. We've been trying to have a date night for months. The kids are upset, too. They haven't seen you much. What are you going to do about it?"

Those Tap-Taps and Knock-Knocks fell on deaf ears. Then the Bang-Bang arrived with the vengence of a Category 4 hurricane.

After a year of working sixty hours a week and training another thirty hours—with a new baby scheduled to arrive within a couple of weeks of my intended departure to climb K2—Meredith was frustrated. While I was slightly concerned, I also wanted to escape life's doldrums and fulfill my dream of climbing K2. So, I stuck to my plan to climb K2, despite anything anyone else wanted from me—and even with the birth of our second son on the horizon.

The Bang-Bang got even louder when I was at Camp 2 on K2. I received a call in the morning. Meredith shared that our newborn, Cortland, had to be admitted to the hospital again. This time was different. He'd been running a fever and was losing weight. He was in potential danger.

Here is some context: Previously, Cortland had been sick, then got better, then sick again, then better again during the first part of the K2 expedition. I asked Meredith if she wanted me to come home during those times, and she said, "No, he'll be fine." So this time was clearly different as he was admitted to the hospital for a recommended five-day stay so that they could run some tests. At this point, I knew it was time to go home. Following the advice of the local leaders, I said I wasn't feeling well and prepared to leave — and my intention to reach the summit. Rather than hiking approximately eighty miles for a week, being "not well or ill," secured a military rescue so I was home in five days rather than ten days or more. That was one of the first steps I took to put my goals aside for the greater good of our family.

But the Bang-Bang messages weren't over, and I began to fear that my response might have been too late.

When I returned from K2 and about three weeks had passed, Meredith told me she had her own K2 and reminded me of how hard it was for her during the whole K2 experience (all the training and then the climb itself). Meredith recommended we go to marriage counseling in order to learn more about ourselves, each other, and our marriage. I was hesitant as this usually lead to bad things, and she could read my consternation. To her credit, she said, "I don't want to use marriage counseling as a way to get a divorce. I want to use it as a way to get us stronger and grow together." This felt good to hear, and I was now on board.

I learned a ton about myself and Meredith during this process. The best performers in the world have coaches so why don't more couples proactively have a marriage coach? One of the takeaways for me was that my passion for mountain climbing had morphed into an obsession, and I had often ignored all other aspects of my life.

Meredith and I had to reassess our marriage and rebuild parts of it. That process continues as I've learned that as two individuals grow and evolve, their relationship must as well. My hunch is that many of us don't do that well. Notice I didn't say change. I think when you say, "you have to change," that has a negative bent, but growth does not. Growth is good. Growth is fantastic. Growth is what life is all about—and it's a never-ending process.

Nate Klemp, who, with his wife, Kaley Klemp, wrote *The 80/80 Marriage: A New Model for a Happier Stronger Relationship*, says there is a new generational challenge that couples are running into, which is really different than couples in the 1950s. "If you look at our generation, in particular, there's this assumption of egalitarian marriage, or in other words, the key question in marriage has become how can we be equals and in love?" he explains. "And the way in which many couples answer that question is through this kind of clunky technology that we call 50-50 Fairness. The idea is we can be equals if we just make everything in marriage — our contributions, the amount of time we spend with various friends and family, the amount of free time we have — perfectly 50-50 fair — and if we do that, then all of a sudden, we ascend to marital bliss, and we never have a problem again."

However, as many of us know, there is never an equal amount of fairness in any relationship — in business or in love.

"50-50 fairness is just a recipe for conflict and resentment. It turns out that we always tend to underestimate our partner's contribution and overestimate our own contribution. So, our assessments of what isn't fair are clouded by all these cognitive biases, which are validated by all sorts of psychology," Nate adds. "And so here we are arguing about fairness, and as a result, it's not a very loving situation, because two individuals are essentially trying to figure out 'How do I win?' instead of asking 'How can we win together?'"

Nate calls this a shift from fairness to radical generosity. "Generosity is by definition unfair," says Nate. "I'm doing more for you than I am for myself. Right. And so, by being trapped in that mindset of fairness, we're negating the possibility of generosity, which is one of the key characteristics of love."

Identifying My Multiple Personas

Ultimately, the key to breaking down and rebuilding is knowing all the different aspects of yourself — how you show up in the world. Our personas control our life. During the breakdown of my marriage, my mountaineering persona had taken over, and all other aspects of who I am were clouded by my obsession to summit big mountains. Husband, father, businessman, philanthropist, and anti-big-government man were all set aside. Instead of tapping into the positive attributes of my mountaineer persona — being fit and charismatic — I slipped into the dark side where my family was an inconvenience.

Luckily, that's changed. Now, I'm determined to see my sons grow up and be there for them — and I don't plan to climb another dangerous mountain again. I find other ways to nurture my mountaineer persona through less extreme climbs.

Identifying different personality traits, attaining awareness of how they control our lives, and engaging them with consciousness allows us to tap into the strengths of our personas without letting the dark sides take over. This is not only healthy for us mentally but physically as well.

Dr. Jeffrey Rediger, author of *Cured: The Life-Changing Science of Spontaneous Healing*, writes, "There is a powerful link between our very identities and our immune systems. Perhaps what ultimately determines the health of the 'soil' of your body is how well you know who you really are at the most authentic level — beneath appearances, 'shoulds,' perceived expectations, and all the masks and roles that you assume for yourself and the world."

> "Identifying different personality traits, attaining awareness of how they control our lives, and engaging them with consciousness allows us to tap into the strengths of our personas without letting the dark sides take over."
>
> −Bo Parfet

As a businessman, I do meticulous research and preparation and am a good negotiator. The dark side of this persona is that I'm a butthead to deal with and make those around me feel like crap. By being aware that I can slip into my nasty dude persona, I catch myself before making unkind remarks or without assessing whether or not there is a win-win scenario I might be overlooking.

My persona as a big game hunter also plays a big role in my life. On the lighter, more positive side, big game hunters are conservationists at heart. Teddy Roosevelt modeled this quite well. Most big game hunters act in alignment with quality animal management guidelines that are put in place to preserve the health of a herd. For instance, hunters in Africa may only target lone male animals, and these are often older animals that attract predators because of their lack of mobility. When they're culled from the herd, there are fewer attacks, and there are more resources for younger, more vital animals who will continue to procreate and perhaps keep a species from extinction. Closer to home, most game is hunted to curb overpopulation.

On the dark side, poachers working to fulfill the desires of those on the black market are an obvious example. To be clear, poaching is not good.

The darker sides of myself (of the personas) had to be acknowledged and released. In other words, a part of me had to die, or the shadow side of my personas would infect all that was right in my life.

> "The darker sides of myself (of the personas) had to be acknowledged and released. In other words, a part of me had to die, or the shadow side of my personas would infect all that was right in my life."
>
> —Bo Parfet

You Must Die Inside

The key to dying inside was letting go of the different personas I donned in each of my relationships and circumstances. To be clear, a persona has both a light and shadow or as some say a positive or negative. It is absolutely ok to be in your negotiator persona when you are buying a car or house. It's probably not ok to be in that mode when you are exploring different vacation options or dinner options with your spouse or children. Also, the trick is to not get stuck in a persona for too long. It's important to be able to pivot between the different ways we relate with others depending on the circumstances in a healthy way, being ever mindful of how our shadow might hijack a situation.

Unfortunately, before I became aware of the existence of these personsa, and their different aspects, instead of listening to my heart and showing up as who I am, that little boy, who always felt like he would never be enough, had to be protected, so my ego took over. I'd show up as the mountaineer. I'd show up as the businessman. I'd put on a different persona to fit my agenda at times, which was often controlled by my ego—that wounded little boy who was still seeking love and approval.

Essentially, I was lost. That's where my personal rebuilding began, by doing inner child work.

Inner child work involves taking a long hard look at the trauma in our childhood that leaves us feeling filled with shame and often mistrustful of those around us.

"To admit as children to oneself that our caregivers will not and do not take care of us, or worse, harm us is akin to emotional suicide," says Shirley Davis, author of "Healing Trauma Through Inner Child Work."

She adds, "Thus, inner children learn to hide their feelings of rejection, experiences of abuse, and fear of abandonment deep inside. Unfortunately, by repressing these intense emotions, adults find themselves stuck in cycles of self-sabotage."

In addition to my earlier young male antics of taking risks while driving, I also was active on the dating scene. My fear of abandonment was running the show at times, and I'd look for a connection, and as soon as things became a little too emotionally intense, I would bail. Through my own emotional unavailability, ironically,

> "Through my own emotional unavailability, ironically, the very thing I was trying to avoid — abandonment — was being repeated over and over."
>
> —Bo Parfet

the very thing I was trying to avoid—abandonment—was being repeated over and over.

"Self-sabotage includes actions against oneself that stop one from achieving the goals one wants, drives away relationships. Self-sabotage convinces you that you do not want these things," says Davis. "Adults who have unresolved inner child pain find themselves seeking out a parent and feel disappointed and rejected when the partner cannot fulfill their demands. On the other end of the stick, survivors may not seek out relationships at all for fear of being hurt again."

Essentially, I needed to look at the losses in my life and heal them myself, without depending on someone outside of myself to fill a hole inside of me—whether that was my father, my mother, the women I'd dated, and even Meredith.

There are a few things I did to heal my inner child. I tapped into things I loved to do as a child. I rekindled an interest in hobbies that I once thought was useless to pursue, such as scuba diving or photography, because I'd been discouraged by a few individuals in my life. I went to workshops and received guidance from mentors, some of whom encouraged me to contact my old girlfriends. Interestingly, this exercise showed me that I wasn't the monster I thought I was and that most of them simply felt that the relationship had run its course and they were ready to move on. Making those phone calls took a boatload of courage. I was afraid they'd confirm the worst of what I felt about myself.

> "Vulnerability is not weakness; it's our greatest measure of courage."
>
> –Brené Brown

Many therapists and lifework mentors advocate viewing pictures of yourself as a child. Some even say to put that photo on your phone's home screen. This serves as a reminder to speak to ourselves kindly. So many of us who have been traumatized are really good at self-bashing.

Reframing our experiences, especially our losses, and learning to love ourselves for who we are takes time, courage, and patience. It is lifelong work. I'm far from done, and I'm committed to breaking down and rebuilding unhealthy behaviors that negatively affect myself and those around me.

Doug Holladay says, "The definition of loss simply means out of place, or not where you should be."

He reminds us that most of us are out of place because we're born into someone else's story—not only the story of our family but also of our culture. This is where our values are defined. We continue to live that story until we have the courage to look at the truth of our own story and ask, "Is this mine?"

Doug says, "We must ask: What am I chasing? Who am I? What am I really looking for?"

I wish I could say that I was alone in these struggles, but I'm not. While writing his book, Doug discovered that in an *Inc* survey before the pandemic—of 3,000 CEOs—over 50% said they were lonely and disconnected. Of the 50%, 61% said they're making bad decisions because they didn't have anyone they trust in their life.

> "To trust others, we must first come to trust ourselves, and that's where radical honesty comes in. We must be courageous enough to look inside and acknowledge what isn't working in our lives."
>
> —Bo Parfet

To trust others, we must first come to trust ourselves, and that's where radical honesty comes in. We must be courageous enough to look inside and acknowledge what isn't working in our lives. We must have the courage to break down the structures that don't serve our higher purpose in life. And that's hard work. It's also frightening. Most of us would rather go along with the status quo than risk losing those we love and respect. Our actions are based on winning the love and approval of others rather than being loyal to the story of our own making—one that is in alignment with our heart's highest purpose.

"In a world where perfectionism, pleasing, and proving are used as armor to protect our egos and our feelings, it takes a lot of courage to show up and be all in when we can't control the outcome," says Brené Brown, in *Atlas of the Heart: Mapping Meaningful Connection and the Language of Human Experience.* "It also takes discipline and self-awareness to understand what to share and with whom. Vulnerability is not oversharing; it's sharing with people who have earned the right to hear our stories and our experiences. Vulnerability is not weakness; it's our greatest measure of courage."

To find that courage, we must learn to retreat into the silence of our hearts. I've been lucky enough to do that while on the mountains, where there are fewer distractions clamoring for my attention. Stepping back to gain a different perspective with all of life pulling at you requires extreme discipline and focus.

Doug hosts silent retreats for many of his clients who are high-performing CEOs. "During the sessions," he says, "They begin to at least understand that there is another space they can go to. It's hard work because as soon as they leave, it's almost like the drug dealers are ready to give them the crack cocaine—accolades, success, money, and power."

For me, my drug has been summiting mountains and feeding my need for extreme adventure.

But over time, I've gained an understanding of the person I've become and the influences around me that serve me or deter me. I've learned to take a stand on what matters most to me. And I've had to surround myself with people who support me rather than drag me down. Doug emphasizes that "high achieving people always want optionality. But what's most important is finding our audience—those who enable us to stand for what is true and right in our life."

He adds, "If you can't point to a time where it costs you something to take a stand, you're done. Whether you go into politics or go into business, you've got to figure out who you are. If not, everybody's going to define you. The Quakers said, 'We should live to please an audience of one. Our deepest core can only be filled by the transcendent, not by these externalities.'"

And I'll continue to take a stand to grow, learn, and evolve as a human being.

Reflection

>> What in your life needs to be broken down and rebuilt?

>> Whose story are you living?

>> What have you taken a stand for?

>> Where do you to take a stand for?

"Some of us think holding on makes us strong, but sometimes it's letting go."

— Herman Hesse, German-Swiss poet, novelist, and painter

CHAPTER 7

KNOWING WHEN ENOUGH IS ENOUGH

In 2005, I was with a team preparing to summit Everest. There was a palpable energy — excitement mixed with an ominous feeling, one that I couldn't shake. Our team was attempting one of the latest summits pushes ever in Mt. Everest's history. We aimed to summit on June 4th or 5th. The monsoon season was closing in fast, which would be trouble. We were also told the Khumbu Icefall (what separates Base Camp from Camp 1) would be closed, leaving us on our own to navigate back down from high on the mountain to base camp. As the day progressed, mixed feelings intensified. Equipment failures were plaguing me. At Camp 2, the zipper broke on my boot, and I had to borrow one that was less than an ideal fit, but at least the zipper closed. About fifty minutes into my summit climb, my head torch went out, and this despite having refreshed the batteries just moments before leaving camp. I had no choice but to follow my Sherpa, who also had to tend to one other climber, one who was falling behind. Then, I was left alone.

I slowly climbed in the darkness, being ever mindful of my steps, as I waited for the Sherpa to return with my fellow climber about 200-300 feet below me. My anxiety level was increasing, and I had to focus on my breath to keep from wasting energy with my rapid breathing. My heart was pounding in my chest, more so than usual. Then the weather deteriorated. The wind picked up, and the snow began. The visibility diminished to where I could barely see a few feet in front of me. But I pushed on.

A while later, I passed Rob Milne and smacked him on the butt with my ice ax. "Hey, we're doing this!" I shouted.

He coughed and said, "Yeah, we are! Isn't this great?"

I continued my climb, committed to continue even though the conditions hadn't improved. About forty-five minutes later, I heard chatter on the radio, like we were in the middle of the war. It was unbelievable. The Sherpas were talking so fast that I couldn't understand what was happening. I decided to hold off on climbing any further until I knew what the commotion was about. In my gut, I knew something wasn't right. I just didn't know what. The snow and wind were increasing in intensity.

A few other climbers joined me, and then we learned that Rob Milne had died. My mind whirled. I had just passed him less than an hour before. My heart rose into my throat, and I choked back a sob. Dying on the mountain is always a possibility. This death hit too close to home. Rob was a friend, and now he was gone.

I was paralyzed in thought, unable to come to a decision of whether to keep climbing or to descend the mountain. Another climber approached, mentioning he'd passed Rob. A moment of reverence followed. The weather continued to worsen, but this fellow climber was undeterred. He climbed on.

Pushing back my emotions and readying to resume my ascent with several other climbers, I began switching my oxygen bottles, and the connector was broken on the full bottle. I had half a bottle remaining but decided to drive to the balcony (about halfway to the summit) without using my oxygen.

"I'm climbing Everest without oxygen! Should I really do this?" I wondered.

Questions arose in my mind, as I reassessed my oxygen situation and the risks of succumbing to high-altitude pulmonary edema or high-altitude cerebral edema. One of my friends had just died, likely due to one of these conditions.

I reached the balcony along with several other climbers. I sat there for what seemed like an hour, contemplating everything that had gone wrong up until that point. That's when I realized nearly every Sherpa had disappeared. And I knew why. Rob's death had shaken their resolve. The Sherpas believe that when Chomolungma, the Goddess of Mount Everest, becomes angry, she seeks vengeance on the climbers. It is also feared that she would likely not be satisfied with just one death — and that she was searching for her next victim.

I looked at my team, who were gung-ho, alpha males lined up to continue the ascent. I said, "Guys, this doesn't feel right to me. I'm headed down." I'd had enough — more than enough. It wasn't my time to summit.

As I descended the mountain, I pondered the prophetic conversation that climbers have before any big climb before leaving base camp. We're often sitting in the tent having our morning tea. We make eye contact with everyone and agree that if any one of us dies or becomes severely injured on summit day, the others are to keep climbing. We're not going to try to save one person's life and possibly kill three more in the process. It's a tough decision and necessary. If someone can be rescued without risking the lives of other team members, then that is a different story.

When I reached Rob's body, I said a prayer for him and tried to close his eyes. They were frozen open, and that eerie image of his lifeless face still haunts me.

Another climber from our team also decided to call it, and before we continued our descent, we rummaged through Rob's pocket for the personal items that his family would want to remember him by. Climbers always have something in our pockets to remind us of our loved ones. As my friend and I moved Rob to the side of the trail, I wondered what might have changed for him if he had known when to say, "Enough is enough."

Holding On Too Tight

Holding on too tight had been one of my biggest flaws. Everything I did came with such intensity. There were times when I didn't know how to let go — nor wanted to. The Tap-Taps, Knock-Knocks, Bang-Bangs that I spoke of in the last chapter drove the lesson home to me that there are times when enough is enough.

One of my mentors, Jim Warner, used the analogy that I'd been gripping a marble so tightly that I was white-knuckling through life. I might have looked like I had it all together, but in reality, fear-induced control drove my life. The traumas of my childhood ruled me and directed my goals. I was far from floating down the river of life. I was determined to make things happen, often no matter what the cost.

Jim saw this in me and challenged me to loosen up. "Whenever you're holding onto something really tightly, picture a marble in your hand and hold the belief that the marble represents what you are holding so tightly. Then imagine loosening your grip just a bit, and then a little more until you can turn your hand over and imagine dropping the marble onto the floor." When I practiced this, I was able to relax and trust that I didn't have to control everything. In fact, I couldn't.

Additionally, I had to develop a deep spiritual practice and become more mindful in my daily activities. Admittedly, being mindful and in the moment was far easier when I was embraced by the majestic energy of the Seven Summits. At home, I was holding on for dear life, where business and family responsibilities tugged at me.

During one of my most gripping moments, my friend, Nate Klemp, asked me to consider the following question: *"How do you cultivate that quality of allowing and letting go in a world where control seems so necessary, and without it, it feels almost dangerous?"*

In my world, control seemed to be the only option. Danger lurked around every corner — in my relationships, in business, and on the mountain. I felt the only way to be safe was to remain vigilant.

"We need to retain control and safety at various points," Nate adds. "It's probably dangerous to totally let go of control in all moments and let life just sweep you away wherever it takes you."

Thankfully, his statement gave me permission, of sorts, to stay in control in some situations and practice surrender in others. Life afforded me many areas to practice knowing when control was called for, as well as to let go and go with the flow.

To develop my discernment, I had to rely more on intuition than logic. This, too, was a practice. Sometimes I was spot on, and

> During one of my most gripping moments, my friend, Nate Klemp, asked me to consider the following question: *"How do you cultivate that quality of allowing and letting go in a world where control seems so necessary, and without it, it feels almost dangerous?"*

sometimes I missed the cues (those Tap-Taps, Knock-Knocks), all together.

Lynn Robinson, an Intuitive Consultant and author of *Put Your Intuition to Work: How to Supercharge Your Inner Wisdom to Think Fast and Make Great Decisions,* asserts we can develop and begin to trust our intuition by keeping an intuitive log. "Throughout the day, I will ask some questions, such as 'Who's the best person to contact about this? What's my right next step? What do I need to know?'" she explains.

She prefers writing her answers by hand rather than on a computer as it activates her right brain (intuition) over her left brain (logic). "Fragments of answers or fragments of information come through very quickly, almost like Googling the question." She often reviews her log to check on the accuracy of her intuition.

"Intuition is a skill that we can all develop and really rely on," adds Lynn. "When we keep a log, we're acknowledging that we value the answers. We're developing that intuitive muscle."

Like many skills, developing our intuition takes practice, and over time, we learn to trust our intuitive hits more and more. The key is to tone down the "noise" from the outside world. Greg Voisen, author of *Hacking the Gap: A Journey from Intuition to Innovation and Beyond,* described his journey in developing his intuition during a particularly challenging time after his eldest son had been diagnosed with Chronic Mylogonic Leukemia.

"Our entire family was immersed in exploring the delicate balance between life and death. We were seeking to find the balance in life between the everyday demands and that place of inner calm that brings real meaning to all of life's experiences," explains Greg. "What we discovered is that the noise from the outside world is so enticing that if you are not incorporating ways to eliminate the noise — through meditation, contemplation, mindfulness, or any technique that is bringing awareness of the 'now' — that this present moment, which is all we ever have in life, will not be fully experienced. And without living in the moment, we cannot hear the voice of wisdom that resides within us. The real purpose of all these techniques is to bring us into this state of awareness. This is when the magic starts to happen!"

Additionally, our ego, which seeks to protect us at all costs, must be put in its place. Unfortunately, our ego operates with data from the past and has no way to step into the unknown without eliciting fear. And when we refuse to go into the unknown, we're usually hanging on too tight.

Greg states that the only way to override the ego is to practice our intuition, and when we do, we'll experience more peace and confidence in making choices and knowing when enough is enough. We'll let go. In essence, the fear of making the wrong move will subside.

"The ego voice brings fear into our life and persuades us to disbelieve in ourselves," says Greg. "Tuning into our intuition and really listening and following the guidance takes an act of 'knowing' that this small voice is true. It requires trust that our soul's voice is providing guidance and direction in our life that will help us achieve our dreams and not douse them."

> "You have to leave the city of your comfort and go into the wilderness of your intuition. What you'll discover will be wonderful. What you'll discover is yourself."
>
> – Alan Alda

Somethings Are Better Left Untouched

The La Ruta Maya Belize Endurance Canoe Race was something I'd had my eyes on for some time, and I invited Richard Wiese on the adventure. Richard and I had just met at The Explorers Club, so it was an opportunity to get to know him better. Jonathan

Leebow, who was my partner in the Gumball 3000 and a friend from high school, was also along. The event was a multiday canoe race — and it didn't go very smoothly. In fact, we almost died.

"We should have never gotten into that situation," says Richard. "I'm not experienced at all in canoeing or paddling. But since I was president of The Explorers Club, I must know what I'm doing, right? That's when my ego got in the way."

I, too, didn't have the necessary experience, but I also didn't know how to let go of this challenge once it came to my attention.

And this is how the event unfolded.

> "The intuitive mind is a sacred gift, and the rational mind is a faithful servant. We have created a society that honors the servant and has forgotten the gift."
>
> — Albert Einstein

We had come upon a section of the river where many boats had turned over. There were a couple of hundred boats in the race. Wisely, Richard said, "Let's pull off and let them all sort themselves out."

A short time later, we navigated through a mild whitewater rapid and pulled up to a tree to rest and assess our next move. Suddenly, the current sucked the whole boat under, with us with it. We were stuck beneath the boat, and Richard was under the water the longest. After the river freed me, I gripped the side of the tree, with Jonathan close by. I stared beneath the surface of the water, worried for Richard's safety. I wondered if a crocodile might have eaten Richard.

"My father was a pilot, and my father always impressed me by putting himself in a bubble of calm whenever emergencies happened," says Richard. "So, I consciously remember thinking, *'Gosh, you probably got about a minute. Get the canoe off your head. Find the light.'*"

Richard did find the light, and then later, rescuers had to tow the canoe out from under what seemed like a maze of endless fallen trees and debris so that we could carry on with our task. We were lucky.

"I replayed that scenario, many, many, many times over, trying to assess what we did wrong and what we shouldn't have done," says Richard. "That could have had a whole other scenario if one of us had gotten our clothes or even a life vest caught in a branch. We didn't fixate too much on that experience at the time, but afterward, I thought, *'Geez, that was stupid!'*"

Once we righted the canoe and gathered our equipment, we began paddling again. Needless to say, we were dead last in that race. The person who was second to last was an older woman with a dog in front of her boat, and she was paddling alone. While we didn't throw in the towel, we let go of any expectations that we were going to win the race. In fact, our first goal was to finish — just not last.

Open to Other Possibilities

Elizabeth Gould reminds us that sometimes letting go of our expectations that things work out a certain way can actually invite other possibilities that might be even better for us.

"Feeling Forwards is about living life as the complete person you have forgotten you already are and not as the person who's just waiting to shine."

She reminds us that we have all the resources within us to do whatever we want. I proved that many times in my earlier climbs when I was ill-equipped and not in the best shape — but I had what I needed to get through my challenges. I guess we can say that I also had the resources to survive the La Ruta Maya. However, in all these challenging situations, I had to let go of the idea of perfection or success. I discovered so much more about myself in the process.

"The magic of life is if we knew exactly how everything would turn out, it would really be pretty boring," says Gould.

I must admit that the allure of many of my adventures is that of really not knowing what might happen — and then testing my ability to read the situation well enough to navigate my way out of difficulties in one piece.

Resistance to Change

While letting go might be the wise move, many of us resist change — or resist giving up on plans we have our hearts set on. We rarely believe that a better way might be possible, so we maneuver through life with our firmly ingrained habits.

Nate Klemp says, "The practice you need is the one you resist. Wherever you are resisting, there is some real juice there. That could pull a lot of growth."

I've deeply resisted what Nate refers to as suburban domesticated life. Admittedly, that's where I've had to let go of my desire to push the precipice of life and my agendas. Instead, I've had to practice embracing the beauty in the mundane. Thankfully, I've come to appreciate having dinner at home with my family and going out with friends as moments of beauty.

> "The practice you need is the one you resist. Wherever you are resisting, there is some real juice there. That could pull a lot of growth."
>
> — Nate Klemp

But still, I have a lot of room to grow. In my conversations with Nate, he reminded me that I often respond to fear with action. A solution to this — and an edge of growth for me — could be around responding to fear with inaction.

"Sometimes, when you're not on the mountaintop, when you're sitting on your couch, feeling inadequate, or feeling there's something wrong with you, there's nothing you can do. That's when we must stay with the experience of the fear itself," says Nate. "We can only move into some of these deeper existential fears through inaction."

Being mindful of my tendencies to respond to fear with action is a practice that will likely follow me for the rest of my life. However, if I'm willing to let go of my knee-jerk response, I'm at least open to other possibilities.

"People who have the hardest time with their own self-worth and self-esteem are very often the people who can't let go. For example, they might say, 'If I don't make it to that summit, something's wrong with me.' They become like puppy dog that won't let go of the toy. They just keep thrashing at it," says April Rinne.

"There comes a point when we need to acknowledge that I put my best foot forward, and I need to let go of the rest. It becomes really clear really fast that one of the earliest hallmarks of wisdom is to be able to do the best job you can and also recognize that you have zero 'right' or entitlement to any particular results of those efforts. And the same holds true for others," says April. "This is 180 degrees opposite to what we're typically taught — that if I do act, then I'm entitled to have a certain outcome of success. There's an element of privilege in that way of thinking."

> "Every person has the right to put their best foot forward. No person has the right to any particular result."
>
> — April Rinne

Letting Go of Old Beliefs and Identities

On a recent trip to Ecuador, I was with a good buddy, Doug Beall. We had two guides as I was ski mountaineering and Doug was climbing. As we skinned up Cayambe, at multiple points, my guide and I had to take off our skis and don our crampons and pull out the ice ax to climb because the pitch was too steep for skinning up. We had about three inches of fresh snow on top of rock-hard ice. Doug and his guide climbed straight up. My guide and I zigzagged on switchbacks with skins on our skis. The distance we had covered was far more than the 5790 meters of this extinct volcano.

At one point, I noticed my guide was really slowing down. He was struggling. It was a tough ascent, and it was getting steeper. During this particular pitch, we should have taken off our skis earlier, and I regretted not being aware of that, especially after he looked at me and asked, "Do you want to ski down from here?"

And I said, "Why?" I was puzzled.

"I'm really tired," and then he repeated. "Do you want to ski down from here?"

If it were twenty years ago, I would have responded with a lot of heat. But I listened to the signs. I wasn't quite ready to say "enough is enough." Discernment is key in knowing when to hold on and when to throw in the towel.

So, I said, "Oh, man, I'm sorry. I'm sorry to hear that you're not feeling well. Tell me more about that."

And he said, "Well, I'm thirsty. I'm hungry. And I'm really tired. My backpack's heavy. So, let's just stop right here. We keep slipping."

"Let's just take a break," I said, and then I gave him a whole package of my energy chews and some of my energy drink. He drank the whole liter. Before we left, something told me that I should take another liter of water. Thankfully, I listened to my intuition.

Then I opened up his backpack, took out this huge, heavy first aid kit, and put it in my backpack. He also had a rack full of climbing gear, and I took that as well. He was just watching me. I put my skis on my backpack and put on my crampons. And I took his crampons out of his pack, and I said to him, "Andres, how are you feeling? You look so much better. I think we're tired because we should have put on our crampons a long time ago, don't you?"

He agreed, and then he said, "We're gonna get more energy." We said a prayer, and he zoned into that prayer, affirming aloud, "God's gonna give us some more energy."

We started climbing. It was amazing. When he slowed down again, I gave him another package of energy chews and more to drink, along with a dose of encouragement. "Andres, we're getting close. You can do this."

Before we climbed, I asked him how many times he had climbed Cayambe, and he replied 40 or 50 times. But, when we reached the summit, he started crying. I hugged him and waited for a moment before asking, "Andres, what? Why are you so emotional? What's going on? You ok?"

And then he answered, "It's my first time to summit."

Mentally, he'd set himself a barrier and figured that people would likely just stop when he wanted to stop. I responded with compassion and understanding, and he was motivated to move beyond his self-imposed limitations.

I trusted my intuition, I let go of my reactive patterns, and I knew he could make it. Maybe he just needed somebody with warm hands and a big heart.

Surrender to a Higher Power

Letting go of expectations and my own agenda has required me to get in touch with something bigger than myself. I frequently feel that presence on the mountain. However, in daily life, it takes practice to set my ego aside and really listen to what I'm being called to do — to let go of my old patterns that prevent me from connecting with others. This simple act of listening allows me to have faith in people doing the right thing, faith in humanity, and the goodness of people — including myself. And when I'm in touch with that higher power, I know I'm in right action.

Reflection

» Where in your life are you holding on too tight?

» Where might life be asking you to let go?

» Where is entitlement clouding your ability to choose the right action?

"Happiness is the ultimate purpose of human existence."

— Aristotle

CHAPTER 8

HOW TO CLAIM HAPPINESS

In December 2020, I was sitting in a hotel room in Florida about to embark on a trip to Ecuador to climb Cayambe. One of my good friends, John Sable, whom I've hiked with, asked: "Remember what you told me when we last went hiking together?"

After searching my memory, I hadn't a clue.

"Enjoy every step."

Those three words came at the perfect time, and something told me to pay attention to that "Tap-Tap." While I love climbing, there's also a lot of pain involved. The body and mind are taxed mightily. The pain can get very intense, and yes, I still choose to engage in that pain. As Rumi says, "The cure for pain is in the pain."

All climbers know there is pain involved in our sport. Reinhold Messner, a renowned Italian climber, said, "I was not driven by pains, but pains are part of the game, especially if you're going to high altitude. The lungs are hurting, the head is pained, the muscles are in pain… I am not searching for it, but I just know it's happening."

> "The cure for pain is in the pain."
> — Rumi

When the call with my friend ended, I reflected upon the pain of every climb, and the one approaching I knew would be no different. Messner said that he became less tolerant of pain as he grew older. I wondered at what point in my life the same would happen to me. I vowed it would not be on this expedition.

Cayambe was not originally part of my plan. I was planning to skin up and ski down Chimborazo, Ecuador's highest peak, with my buddy Doug, but our plans shifted after that mountain was closed when an avalanche killed six climbers. Not to be deterred, we set our sights on Cayambe, the third highest peak in Ecuador. This extinct volcano is capped with sweeping glaciers, and while not as technical and difficult as Chimborazo, it would still be an adventure—and bring on its own level of pain.

So, heeding those three words *"Enjoy Every Step,"* I made a choice to embrace the pain and find happiness in every single step. After all, I chose this sport—with all the joys and pains involved, even with the possibility of the death of myself or my dear friends.

A few days later, I was skinning up Cayambe and knew that my resolve to enjoy the climb was being tested. As my quads started to burn, I would say to myself, "My quads need a break; thanks for letting me know." I then switched muscles and used mainly my glutes to propel me upward. Then when the glutes tired, I would switch hamstring and the calves. I would continue these rotations. If I felt out of breath, I would stay to myself, "Great. Thanks for letting me know; let's do some sets of pressure breathing." Twelve hours of climbing had never felt better.

A mindset shift was in order. What I did was search to find joy in every step, knowing that I could. That's where I disagree with Reinhold Messner. With the right mindset, pain can be turned into pleasure.

My gratitude practice kicked into gear. I pivoted from focusing on the pain in my quads and glutes to appreciating the hard work my muscles were doing to make this climb possible. I expressed gratitude for the rocks along the trail, the view of the peaks and valleys around me, and every sip I took from my energy drink.

The pain became a distant memory, and once again, I was completely in the moment, absorbed in the beauty around me.

I chose happiness and found joy in every step.

Enjoy Every Step

All aspects of life require us to engage in a process, and while I've not always enjoyed the process, I know mountains are not climbed, businesses are not started or saved, and relationships do not become closer without both joy and pain. Yet, the more we lean into the experiences and open our arms to all that these moments bring to our lives, the more rewards we reap on the other side of challenges. The strife that whirls inside of us or between ourselves and others can be a catalyst to bring more happiness, joy, and contentment to our lives.

Martin Seligman, a pioneer in positive psychology, breaks down happiness into three measurable components: pleasure, engagement, meaning. Essentially, happiness is the joy we feel striving after our potential.

Be in Charge of Your Own Happiness

Over the years, I've learned that turning to others for the source of my happiness leads to misery. While my childhood was difficult, it likely prepared me to strive to be the source of my own contentment and joy in life.

Now, this doesn't mean I don't need other people. I love my wife and my sons. I value the relationships with my fellow climbers and my business colleagues. I'm not ready to be a hermit. However, I truly believe that we cannot find joy searching for validation from the people around us, nor in filling others' needs through our co-dependent actions.

I think one of the best practices for a happy, healthy marriage is to be in charge of your own happiness.

According to the National Center for Health Statistics, a division of the Center for Disease Control and Prevention, while divorce rates have been decreasing alongside marriage rates, there are 2.3 divorces per every thousand marriages. This figure doesn't even take into account the number of long-term monogamous relationships among non-married couples that have dissolved. My bet is that many of these relationships failed because one or perhaps both of the people were seeking to fill a hole inside themselves and looking to the other person to be the solution. That is not a path to success, but one that leads to a major failure. I know that from my earlier dating years, and I also experienced that with Meredith.

> "I've learned that turning to others for the source of my happiness leads to misery."
>
> — Bo Parfet

Rarely has there been a time when my travel schedule hasn't posed a significant challenge in my marriage. Early on, I was on the road 250 days a year, and she essentially felt stuck in Michigan—where she was working for my father's business and didn't know many people. Admittedly, she was disappointed that we didn't spend more time together.

However, one of the ways we make it work is to tend to our own happiness as well as cultivate the happiness that our boys feel in their lives. Meredith has always had her own interests, so she was not left waiting. Prior to moving to Kalamazoo for our relationship, she was working on global HIV projects and traveling all over the developing world helping train physicians and improve care in rural clinics.

But it is her search for meaning beyond accomplishments that has helped her feel fulfilled. Her sister's death, as well as her own near-death experience, sparked a mindfulness practice that later led her to become a death doula and hospice chaplain, both of which bring her great joy and purpose. In doing this work, she brought to my attention two concepts: contemplative happiness and conventional happiness. Recently in the magazine, *Mindful,* she wrote an article which described conventional happiness as the distractions we turn to, such as "social media, binging shows, shopping, eating, drinking, gossiping—anything that mutes painful feelings."

She also shared the definition of contemplative happiness as defined by David Chernikoff, an early leader in the US hospice movement, meditation teacher, and author of *Life, Part Two,* as "a sense of awareness and contentment that doesn't rely on external circumstances to make us feel happy."

Essentially, we must turn away from outside distractions to truly know what brings us joy, happiness, and contentment. Then we must build these activities or ways of being into our daily lives.

Shifting Your Happiness Set-Point

Marci Schimoff, the author of *Happy for No Reason: 7 Steps to Being Happy from the Inside Out,* reports that "Researchers have found that no matter what happens to you in life, you tend to return to a fixed range of happiness. Like your weight set-point, which keeps the scale hovering around the same number, your happiness set-point will remain the same unless you make a concerted effort to change it.

And that's the key; we can change our happiness set-point by developing new habits.

Schimoff believes that we can become Happy for No Reason, which she defines as "true happiness — a neurophysiological state of peace and well-being that *isn't* dependent on external circumstances." And she offers three guiding principles which make this possible.

"Guiding Principle #1 — What Expands Makes You Happier. When your energy expands, you experience greater happiness; when your energy contracts, you experience less happiness."

My energy expands when I'm in nature and contributing to people's happiness and well-being through my business ventures. It expands when I'm spending time with my family. It contracts when I'm with people who blame and complain about themselves, other people, and the world. (More on that in a moment.)

"Guiding Principle #2 — The Universe is Out to Support You." When you believe that the universe is out to support you, you're able to stop resisting what is happening. This doesn't mean being passive or complacent about the events in the world or in your life. It simply means stop fighting or bemoaning *what has already happened* and can't be changed."

I haven't always been able to feel that the universe had my back, particularly during the failure of Jumar. In hindsight, I have seen the silver lining. On a daily basis, it takes practice to see that plane delays, traffic jams, and even disagreements with my family or colleagues might just be working to bring about some greater good in my life.

"Guiding Principle #3 — What You Appreciate, Appreciates. "Whenever you appreciate the happiness that already exists in your life, like money in the bank, appreciates."

Again, it boils down to looking at what is working well in our life — and expecting that to continue.

Remember the wise words of Meister Eckert, "If you can only learn one prayer, make it this one: Thank you."

Don Wenner, founder and CEO of DLP Capital, spearheaded an initiative to help others change their happiness set point and end the happiness crisis. To achieve a work/life integration, a situation that when out of balance often throws us into unhappiness, we must address what Don refers to as the Personal Compass made of 8Fs: Faith, Family, Fitness, Finance, Fulfillment, Freedom, Friends, and Fun. The idea is to get as many points in an activity (one for each F) as possible. So, if I take a hike with my family, I've achieved at least four Fs — family, fun, fitness, and fulfillment. If we say a prayer of gratitude on the mountain, that brings us to five.

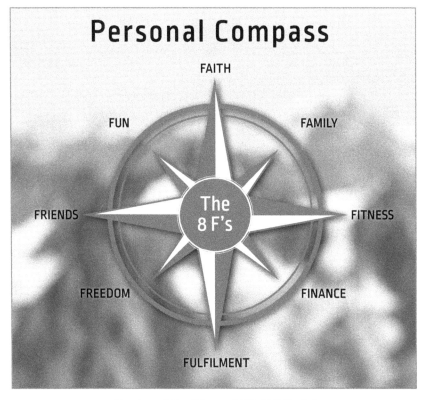

Courtesy of Don Wenner, CEO, DLP Capital

We can adopt a few more habits to change our happiness set-point, so read on.

Smile

There are rare moments when I'm not smiling. When I have pasted a frown on my face, often due to, in April Rinne's words, "mountains that I didn't choose but were put before me," my world contracts. I feel worthless and hopeless. The opposite is also true; sunshine abounds when I can smile no matter what is happening in my life.

In his TedTalk, "The Hidden Power of Smiling," Ron Gutman, founder and former CEO of HealthTap, shared research that proves that smiling is a superpower that is contagious and not only improves the quality of our state of being but it affects those around us, uplifting them and making them feel more positive toward us.

"Smiling can actually make you look good in the eyes of others," he said. "So whenever you want to look great and competent, reduce your stress, improve your marriage, or feel as if you just had a whole stack of high-quality chocolate without incurring the caloric cost, or as if you found 25 grand in a pocket of an old jacket you hadn't worn for ages, or whenever you want to tap into a superpower that will help you and everyone around you live a longer, healthier, happier life, smile."

And when you add laughter, our world brightens even more. The idea is not for what is funny but look for what is genuine and true. Leaders who incorporate humor and laughter into their company cultures and personal lives enhance their well-being and those around them.

According to Naomi Bagdonas, a lecturer at Stanford's Graduate School of Business, "Leaders with a sense of humor are seen as 27 percent more motivating and admired. Their employees are 15 percent more engaged. Their teams are more than twice as likely to solve a creativity challenge."

Get Outside Every Day

It's no secret that I love being outside, and fortunately, so do Meredith and our boys. While they might not be interested in extreme sports, we do enjoy getting out in the mountains of Colorado for a healthy dose of fresh air and exercise.

Too many of us spend long hours glued to our computers and TVs without the benefits of what Richard Louv refers to as "Vitamin N." In one of his blogs, "Ten Reasons Why Children and Adults Need Vitamin N," he writes, "Nature can reduce depression and improve psychological well-being. Researchers in Sweden have found that joggers who exercise in a natural green setting feel more restored and less anxious, angry, or depressed than people who burn the same number of calories jogging in a built urban setting."

Michelle Kondo, a research social scientist with the USDA Forest Service's Northern Research Station, said, "There are many physical and psychological benefits of nature that scientists have observed, which can better help us understand how nature supports wellness in the body, mind and community." Additionally, life expectancy increases, sleep quality improves, cancer risk decreases increasing, and motivation is enhanced according to Kondo.

Building a habit of stepping out of the house or office every day is important. Sometimes there isn't time for a hike, but the boys and I might throw a football, bounce on the trampoline, or simply take a walk in the park looking at the flowers and trees. Slowing down and being aware of the beauty of nature in my own backyard is how I bring the mountains home with me.

Set Boundaries with Toxic People

Jim Rohn, an American entrepreneur and motivational speaker, said, "You are the average of the five people you spend the most time with." Choosing who is in your circle is important if you are to be happy and successful.

We all have been around people who drain us and even infect us with their foul moods. Many times, we can avoid spending time with those people altogether. Yet, sometimes we have to compromise for the greater good.

For instance, Meredith loves to spend two to four weeks (in a row) at her mother's place in the mountains in Colorado. This is great for Meredith and fills her cup with joy and love. Our two boys love it there, too. For me, the right time amount of time is about three days. For us, this works great. We respect the "time limits" with each other's parents. I support her going for a long period of time, and she supports the time I spend there, which fills my cup with love and joy. I often see in underdeveloped couples that they want (or demand) their spouse come stay with their family the "whole time" even though it doesn't feel good to that spouse. Subsequently, the overlooked (or not seen) spouse has resentment, and over time this doesn't bode well for their relationship. A best practice is to feel seen, heard, and supported by your spouse — and also to express your needs respectfully.

Compromise is necessary for happiness to prevail. One of the lessons I learned from the teachings of Les Brown is, "When things go wrong, don't turn on each other, turn to each other." This is just one way we turn to each other, supporting one another while honoring our individual needs and desires.

Creating greater awareness about the people in your life doesn't have to be an ordeal. In fact, it can be accomplished quite simply. In his Breakthrough to Success training, Jack Canfield advises participants to make a list of all the people in their lives. Then next to their names, place a plus sign, a minus sign, or both if the individual can be a mix of both positive and negative influences on us. The next step is to reduce the amount of time or even eliminate the people who have been assigned the minus sign.

I've discovered that negative, small-minded people talk about why things are bad and never mention solutions. Winners point out areas for improvement—and back it up with two or three potential solutions. There's often a great divide between these two camps.

In "How to Escape the Cynicism Trap," psychologist and neuroscientist Jamil Zaki says that "Some days, it's hard to be optimistic. But cynicism—the idea that people are inherently selfish, greedy, and dishonest—is making humanity lonelier and more divided."

We can see evidence of that all around us—in the news, in our offices, and even in our homes.

Zaki adds, "Cynicism is not the only root of our problems, and optimism alone will not fix them. But it's hard to change a broken system if you think it's a mirror reflecting our broken nature. If people are selfish to our core, then toxic laws and practices are here to stay. But we can all choose to tell a different story. We can be skeptical—demanding evidence before we believe in people—but hopeful, knowing they can change for the better. We can find other people in our neighborhoods, unions, and faith communities who want the same thing. We can use our collective optimism to build pockets of solidarity and mutual aid."

The key is taking responsibility. However, Gary Vaynerchuk, commonly known as Gary Vee, a Belarusian-American entrepreneur, author, speaker, and Internet personality, believes the lack of responsibility and accountability is one of the worst plagues in our society. "We are now the finger-pointing generation... People would rather complain about how it is rather than put in the work." But he explains that when we take responsibility for the conditions in our life, without beating ourselves up, we are liberated. "When you lean into accountability, your life gets happier!" he exclaims.

As for bringing more positive energy into our life, we can make a list of people we perceive to be positive influences and strive to spend more time with them. Jason Valadao makes an effort to engage in meaningful conversations with people on a regular basis, either those he's known for years, needs to reconnect with, or individuals he's just met. He even has a column in his journal to track these conversations, reminding him of the value he's received—and given—as well as ensuring that this aim doesn't fall by the wayside.

The Importance of Friendships

Having like-minded people around me is vitally important. I thrive when I have climbing buddies, friends to have dinner with, and those heart-to-heart chats over a cup of coffee or an adult beverage. In the blog "Friends Nourish the Body and Soul," the Blue Zones group, noted that a "Cornell University polled 100 people in 2011 and found the average American had only two friends with whom they would confide important, personal matters. During times of high stress, friendships have a tendency to fade into the background, while work and family take center stage, battering themselves into the foreground of our lives.

Additionally, "Research shows this is a mistake and in fact, counterproductive to maintaining your physical, mental, and emotional well-being. Here are some consequences of social isolation and a few tips on how to build and keep the right tribe to improve your health, happiness and even life expectancy."

Fewer friends mean negative physical and mental effects, increased mortality, and increased risk of chronic conditions.

Blue Zones also noted, "The mortality risk for people who find themselves socially isolated is equal to that caused by obesity and physical inactivity. Having close relationships, in fact, increases your life span at a rate equal to that of quitting smoking. Dr. James House at the University of Michigan found the chance of dying over a period of 10 years increases by 10 percent for people who live alone or have only a few friends compared to people with more friends and family."

Additionally, former surgeon general of the United States, Vivek H. Murthy, writes, "Loneliness and weak social connections are associated with a reduction in lifespan similar to that caused by smoking fifteen cigarettes a day and even greater than that associated with obesity."

Ensuring that I have meaningful memories with my boys is crucial. After reading the book, *The Family Board Meeting: You Have 18 Summers to Create Lasting Connection with Your Children* by Jim Shiels, I've adopted the practice of having a family board meeting with each of my sons. It's vital that they know I see and hear them for who they are. In addition to our family board meetings, I take a special trip each year with each of my sons. We often combine the family board meeting with the father-son trips. This year they asked for a trip for the three of us together, and I made it happen. I'm committed to strengthening our father-son bond to lessen the chance of them going through the inner challenges I've had to face. While I know they'll have their own lessons, I can at least do my best in this arena for them.

Strive for Balance

While setting goals and fulfilling our missions is important, doing so without sacrificing the other areas of our life is also essential. At times, balance can be difficult to achieve, as I've proven when training for one of my expeditions.

To achieve balance, Marcus Baur cautions us not to take anything for granted. Again, gratitude for all that we have in our lives is key.

Additionally, Marcus says, "We have 7.9 billion people on this planet, and the challenge we face is achieving true happiness that doesn't require endless resource spending. We must learn to balance our inner world and our outer world."

In other words, more isn't always better. Contentment with what we already have achieved or possess is key to our peace and well-being. That's where social media can be our nemesis. It's easy to see other people presenting their "ideal" lives, but what we rarely see is the real story behind many of their posts.

April Rinne says, "It does seem that humanity is in a heckuva tough place when it comes to our obsession with 'more.' We want more money, more power, more likes, more clicks, more clothes, *more everything*. Moreover, more is what leads to comparison with others. To fear. To self-doubt.

"In so many ways, chasing 'more' in the outside world leaves us feeling empty inside. It burns up the planet at the same time that it burns a hole through our pocketbooks and burns us out. More is *not* inherently better. It's actually a vicious, icky, and thankfully human-made cycle."

Achieving contentment with what we already possess, whether material possession or accolades, might take a change in our outlook.

Richard Wiese says having the right perspective is necessary. "I know more unhappy people because all their friends are going skiing in Aspen, and they're stuck at home. Or they feel that they're not fulfilled because they don't have certain material items. While I like nice things, and I have the latest iPhone, I don't necessarily need them to be happy."

He also believes breaking out of our bad habits and nurturing relationships is important.

"Our relationships have become so transactional, especially when distance is involved. I'd like to make more of an effort with those relationships rather than get stuck in a rut and turn on the TV when the workday is done. It's nice to have that buddy you can call up, knowing they're not going to judge you. I think that's what I witness in the villages I visit filming *Born to Explore*. People have their aunt, uncle, brother, and sister. There's somebody who knows them, and so I think there's a lot less anxiety. The difference between want and need is easily seen in these situations."

Keep Growing

Continuous learning is important to me. I listen to podcasts and audiobooks, spend time with mentors, and more. I want to grow into the best possible person I can be.

Gretchen Rubin, the author of *The Happiness Project*, says, "To feel happy, we need to feel growth—a sense of learning, of betterment, of advancement, of mastery, of contributing to the growth of others of fixing things, improving things, making things better, assuming responsibility. Growth helps to explain the happiness brought by children, by gardens, by pay raises, by stamp collections, by training for a marathon or cleaning out the garage or volunteering to get the finances organized at a local non-profit."

Growing takes effort, and often times we want the fast-food approach to happiness, but that often doesn't last.

Jim Hobbs, Chief Longevity Officer at The Adventure Life Project, says, "Pleasure and enjoyment have become cheap and easy, for most, and for many the default. Conversely, achieving a state of flow requires some thought and some effort and is usually packaged as a challenge. We have been conditioned to avoid challenges whenever possible, and in so doing, we avoid the very opportunities to learn, improve, and excel. We avoid the one thing, the stepping-stone that can get us to a state of flow–excitement."

And, of course, by now, you know that I strive to learn more about myself with each step on the mountain—and off.

Cultivate Awe

Awe can be invited into our lives as well. I'm often overtaken by the feeling of the magnificence all around me while climbing. Many of us who are called to the mountains feel the same. And a fun fact to note is that Nepal was ranked #84 as the happiest country in South Asia by the *World Happiness Report.*

Richard Wiese says he's in a near-constant state of awe, no matter where he is.

"Part of my maturation as an explorer, a parallel of evolving as a human being as well, is that I'm finding a lot about happiness; I can be happy. I live along the water in Connecticut. There's a tidal flat where I go out and peer at little snails or currents of eddies of waters. I find it very beautiful and interesting. If I spot a unique animal pawprint or a bird, I'm pretty jazzed about it," Richard says.

"I've been to Antarctica; I've been to Everest. I've been to Kilimanjaro and the North Pole. I've been to a lot of places that have been absolutely breathtaking. But I've been able to dial it back in and create happiness or curiosity, no matter where I am. I could be waiting for my kids to come out of basketball practice, and if I saw a hawk or an eagle fly by, I'd be like, 'Oh, wow.'"

> "Experiences of wonder are often ephemeral in duration but can be everlasting in effect."
>
> — Jeffrey Davis, author of *Tracking Wonder: Reclaiming a Life of Meaning and Possibility in a World Obsessed with Productivity*

Again, slowing down to observe our surroundings is what it takes to experience awe and be open to what we might not ordinarily see when we have blinders on to navigate through our busy schedules.

Serve Others

When our life has a purpose, and our success is built around our passions, we find meaning, and meaning goes beyond happiness. And while I'll share more about this in the next chapter, Meredith and I formed Denali Venture Philanthropy to support advocacy and education around impact investing and to fund entrepreneurs who are committed to social change.

However, serving others does not always mandate a financial investment. Our time is just as, if not more, valuable. Serving is about sharing kindness with our fellow human beings. And it seems pandemics and other global tragedies actually bring out the best in us.

Vicki McKeever, a reporter for CNBC, reported that the United Nations Sustainable Development Solutions Network's 10th World Happiness Report "noted a global upsurge in benevolence in 2021, amid the Covid-19 pandemic…John Helliwell, a professor at the University of British Columbia who helped edit the report, said there had been a 'remarkable worldwide growth' in the three acts of kindness measured by the Gallup World Poll: helping strangers, volunteering, and donations. People were doing all three nearly 25% more than before the pandemic, he pointed out.'"

We can make a difference in others' lives in simple ways, from buying a cup of coffee for the person standing behind us in line at our favorite coffee shop to handing out socks to the homeless people in the neighborhood park. Often, we benefit from these acts of kindness more than we realize, and in this, we create significance.

Victor Frankl, psychiatrist, Holocaust survivor, and author of *Man's Search for Meaning*, discovered that even in the direst circumstances, we can positively influence another's life, and from that, we can find meaning.

"The one thing you can't take away from me is the way I choose to respond to what you do to me. The last of one's freedoms is to choose one's attitude in any given circumstance," he says.

And where we find freedom, we find happiness.

Reflection

» How might you take charge of your own happiness?

» What people have you identified as toxic, and how might you limit the time spent with them or eliminate them altogether?

» How might you increase your happiness set-point?

"Success is about
us. Significance
is about others."

— John C. Maxwell

CHAPTER 9

FROM SUCCESS TO SIGNIFICANCE

Early on in my climbing tenure, I set out to reach goals, but that wasn't the only reason. With each expedition, I committed my climb to raising money for charities, for participating in scientific studies, and for writing books that inspire people to make changes in their lives.

I often get asked, "How do I have so much energy?" and "How do I get more energy and meaning in my life now that I am retired or sold my business?"

Well, one way to create huge amounts of energy for yourself (and others) and attract more meaning into your life is to create layers with one experience. Let me give you a few examples:

As part of my second climb up Kilimanjaro, we teamed up with The Explorers Club and a biotech company to look for life forms in extreme environments. In scientific terms, we would say let's go "bioprospecting for extremophiles."

Kilimanjaro is an extreme environment—think jungle to high alpine desert to glaciers to high altitude with little oxygen and intense ultraviolet light. We were trained to be scientific field researchers. This was awesome! We took a bunch of soil samples during the climb up Kilimanjaro and discovered 29 new species!

We also raised money to put more poor Africans through medical school. So, this one experience has many "delicious layers of the cake of life."

Additionally, I am on the Advisory Board of Adventure Scientists®, a nonprofit organization partners scientists with outdoor adventurists to collect environmental data to find solutions to the climate crisis and other environmental challenges. This organization was founded by Gregg Trennish, who is also the executive director. Gregg was named *National Geographic Explorer* of the year in 2008. To be a small part of this amazing organization is remarkable. We are working on the Timber Tracking Project, to "enforce anti-poaching regulations, improve forestry management practices, and plan for climate change impacts." We're also underway with the Wild and Scenic Rivers project which "addresses water quality data gaps and update the status of Wild and Scenic Rivers across the nation, improving how these river systems are managed and protected."

So, adding layers to one experience creates more energy, more joy and more impact on the world. And you just might inspire someone to do the same.

Moving Beyond Happiness

While I strive to enjoy each day and each step on the mountain, I realize that being on this earth demands that we reach for more than just enjoying the moments in our day. We're put on this earth to make a difference in others' lives. And to do that, we must know our purpose, and before we can even decide what that is, we need to know what matters to us. Identifying our values makes that possible. Here are mine:

Grit, Passion, and Perseverance toward long-term goals.

Living Fully: The quest for excellence and the pursuit of my passions applies to all aspects of my life — business, family, personal, and faith. I strive to live life to the fullest.

Twenty-Mile March: I consistently hit targets, day after day, year after year, regardless of the prevailing conditions.

Humble Confidence: I exude confidence without arrogance, projecting humility and warmth to empower others and emphasize collaboration.

Servant Leadership: I serve God, my family, and my communities through my work and impact entities with a Servant's heart and spirit.

Impact: We focus our giving on causes. We can leverage our time, talent, treasures, and platform to make a significant impact. We focus on providing a hand-up.

When we're clear about our values and how we're living our values, our lives matter; however, it's easy for our attention to slip away from maintaining a commitment to living our values unless they are constantly front of mind. Journaling is one way to ensure that our daily actions match what we say is most important to us. It's hard to ignore how we might have missed opportunities to be in the right action when we do daily check-ins with ourselves.

James Clear, author of *Atomic Habits: An Easy & Proven Way to Build Good Habits & Break Bad Ones,* says, "Each year, I conduct an Integrity Report. This report has three sections. First, I list and explain my core values. Second, I discuss how I have lived and worked by those core values over the previous year. Third, I hold myself accountable and discuss how I have missed the mark over the previous year and where I did not live up to my core values."

Once we're clear about our values, we can then explore our purpose — that which not only brings meaning to our lives, but it also enhances others by providing a "hand-up."

In her TED Talk, "There's More to Life than Being Happy," Emily Esfahani Smith says, "Finding your purpose is not the same thing as finding a job that makes you happy. Purpose is less about what you want than about what you give. A hospital custodian told me her purpose is to heal sick people. Many parents tell me, 'My purpose is raising my children.' The key to purpose is using your strengths to serve others. Of course, for many of us, that happens through work. That's how we contribute and feel needed. But that also means that issues like disengagement at work, unemployment, and low labor force participation — these aren't just economic problems; they're existential ones, too. Without something worthwhile to do, people flounder. Of course, you don't have to find purpose at work, but purpose gives you something to live for."

Unfortunately, many of us lose sight of what success means to us and fall back on the societal norm of success. Doug Holladay believes the cultural definition of success has been formulated and reinforced, and that leaves people empty and wanting. "You could translate that to almost any field, whether it's mountain climbing, professional athletics, or in business or politics. At some point, you have to address your limitations, and those limitations go up. No one can evade the limitation. No one can skirt around the inevitable — the inevitable is that people can't climb another mountain, or they're no longer going to be asked to be CEO. They're no longer going to be the best politician to be the candidate for president," he shares. "The problem at the heart of all this is defining your identity in the wrong way. And you're defining your identity by extrinsic things rather than intrinsic to who you are. This is why to me, success is an intensely spiritual quest. If you're a human doing, you have to keep doing to be validated. If you're a human being, that is a very, very different way you think about yourself. It's about taking a stand for what you believe in rather than what's expected of you. And it's much easier when you've received a blessing of an elder."

Many of us who climb have taken that role of becoming an elder and seek to positively impact those around us with our wisdom and knowledge. In part, that's why this book is being written. We see people who have struggled as we have and seek to raise them. To do that, the bar of our success must continually rise.

Jason Valadao, MD believes winning and being at the top is great—but there is so much more. "It's not about climbing that summit or making money. What matters is to be as good as we can be because we are as human beings, and we're given this opportunity," says Jason. "I look at life as this: I am able to get up and breathe. I want to make the most of today. I want to fit in as much as I can today."

Elizabeth Gould reminds us that often when we've achieved success, there's a downward turn in our emotions—the post-success blues. That time when we lose sight that all we've been immersed in has a greater meaning than just reaching a goal.

"What we forget is that it's not merely about the achievement. It's how that contribution is going to affect you and affect those around you," says Elizabeth. "If your goal is to win a gold medal, for example, because you want to inspire people that have come from a similar underprivileged background or a certain ethnicity, or you're the first person in your hometown to win a gold medal or whatever else, that is a bigger aim than the goal of winning a gold medal, and that will sustain you. That also shapes life beyond a gold medal and a best-selling book, which are just markers. In the journey of life, it's not an endpoint. It's not even a resting place. Life is about continually moving forward and evolving—and modeling that to those around you."

Claudia Schiepers concurs that our endeavors must include adding value, and if that's missing in life, that's when we feel like we have to go find another adventure. "I still like to think that I can add value and that gives me more satisfaction than anything else," Claudia says, adding that she continually assesses if she is indeed making positive changes to those around her. "I ask, 'Did the company change, or am I having a positive influence on the culture of the company?' If I have, that gives me a lot of satisfaction." And that to her is success.

Lynne Twist and Sara Vetter of The Soul of Money Institute believe that success comes from saying yes to a cause or task or organization that "fuels us rather than depletes us, and it's sourced from our heart's desire to offer our life to something larger than ourselves," they say. "As we move into inspired and committed action, we become the conduit for something that wants to happen in the world. To live a committed life is to be a steward of transformation. Transformation does not deny the past or insult the present. Instead, it is an energetic field that is activated by a vision for a new possibility for yourself, your life, and the world."

Jamie Wheal claims that once you surrender to your dharma or your purpose, the idea is to let yourself be consumed by your dedication to that which is yours to do — that in itself is an act of growing up — and a great act of service, inspiring hope and change to others.

To offer hope to others, though, requires that we believe in the power of community.

The Power of Community

During my worldwide travels, I witnessed powerful community bonds within the cultures in and around the mountain villages. The sense of family and of everyone working together for the common good was palpable in most instances (and yes, there have been some harrowing experiences as well). It's likely why so many of us go back—not only for the climb—but for the connections and the feeling of being welcomed wholeheartedly by people who have so little in terms of material possessions but are wealthy beyond what many in the so-called first world experience in their own lives.

Richard Wiese's purpose and passion have revolved around exploring and experiencing cultures around the world. He says, "In the very first world environment or society, there's this mythical creature called happiness, and everybody is searching for what's going to fulfill them or make them happy. People never were on their deathbed saying, 'Oh, I should have bought that red Ferrari. In the end, you're surrounded by those who are closest to you. A sense of community is so important. And time and time again, wherever I've been, there may be people who don't have a collectively great existence, but that existence has always been better because and safer and less anxious because they had their community with them."

He discovered that while there are close to 6,000 languages spoken on Earth, "There are certain universal languages that everyone identifies with—music, art, dance, food, nature that create a collective experience."

Richard, too, has noted that most people, no matter where they live, what language they speak, or their level of income, have common desires. "I've found out that being poor doesn't mean stupid; it doesn't mean you don't have dreams or aspirations. People's goals, whether they're from Pakistan or in a village in Africa, are pretty much the same: provide for their family security, live in a safe environment, and all of those kinds of things," he explains. "I remember talking to an Aboriginal man in Australia, one of the last remaining in the Northern Territory, and he said his observation on the West is 'You're always trying to change the tide of nature. You try to change the course of rivers and eat things out of season.' The Aboriginal people stay very much in the rhythm of nature. They're following its cycles instead of creating other ones."

That sense of being in the rhythm of nature forges a stronger bond within the communities. People come together to raise food, not just for their own families but for their extended families and neighbors as well.

In mountaineering, there is a strong sense of community amongst the climbers. Like any activity, it's formed around like-mindedness, passion for the sport, and also a collective perception that we really are in this life together.

For Dierdre Wolownick, her passion for climbing led to gaining confidence in herself, and in doing so, she's been an inspiration for many men and women who may have once thought certain aspirations were impossible because of their age. She also found a community for the first time in her life, something that became very apparent on her 70th birthday climb on El Capitan.

"I've never really had that kind of solidarity in my life. Normally with climbing, when I go out with my friends or to Alex's house, I'm tagging along because I'm the slowest. I'm the oldest. I'm just out there trying to keep up with everybody," she shared. "But that day on El Cap, everybody was there for me, and there was none of that trying to keep up."

> "If you can inspire one or two people in a good way, then you can inspire the world."
>
> — Nims Purja

By allowing herself to receive the celebration of her accomplishments, Dierdre in turn, gave a gift to those who wanted to honor her on her special day—and she further inspired those who witnessed all of her successes.

Connections can also be quite unexpected when traveling the road of our successes. Richard describes the time he was working with an IMAX crew on the filming of the 10th anniversary of the *Into Thin Air* accident, and he was shown the Director's Cut of the movie. "Within that film, the most gut-wrenching, perhaps even the most private section was when one of the climbers was pinned to the top, and he was talking to his pregnant wife. She knew he was going to die. He knew he was going to die. They were talking about what they would name that daughter. That was pretty profound," he shares.

"Later that day, I was playing cards with a friend of mine in the tea house, and a blonde girl tapped on my shoulder and says, 'Do you mind if I play?' It was unusual to see a little blonde girl at such a high altitude. So, I said to her, 'What are you doing here?' And she said, 'Oh, I'm visiting my daddy's grave.'"

This little girl was the climber's daughter. Richard then had an epiphany: sometimes our expectations are far exceeded by chance encounters. "I realized what you think is going to be the most memorable experience, like reaching the summit, often is not. *It's most likely the people you meet along the way,*" he explains. "I've noticed time and time again that it's the people that have made all the difference in the world—to make travel exciting, expeditions exciting, and jobs exciting."

Connecting with communities on expeditions also raises awareness and desire to be better and do better once we've returned home. Kenton Cool noticed that shift within himself, as well as realized that our forced connectivity through laptops and phones lacks depth. "We have lost face-to-face connectivity with our peers, with our colleagues, and with our community. But climbing gives us that, or adventure gives us that when we are off-grid in Antarctica or high on Everest or on K2—wherever we are, we are forced to take a step back," he explains. "We play card games, we play board games, and we talk to one another when we get up in the morning. We sit down and have a meaningful dialogue. Now honestly, hand on heart, when was the last time you had a meaningful dialogue face to face? It doesn't happen that much anymore. That's why when I come back from expeditions, I've made pledges to myself. I'm going to be a better person, a better father, a better husband—and I ask to be reminded when I'm falling short of that endeavor."

Giving Back

Like Meredith and I, many of my colleagues have made a commitment to giving back to the communities that have given so freely to us. Many have created foundations to channel equipment, food, medical supplies, and more to positively impact the people in the mountain regions.

With an affinity for the people in Uganda, Alison Levine formed the Climb High Foundation, which is dedicated to training local women as porters and trekking guides. These skills allow the women to earn a sustainable living wage to feed their families, access medical care, and provide their children with an education.

> "A man's job is to make the world a better place to live in, so as far as he is able — always remembering the results will be infinitesimal — and to attend to his own soul."
>
> — Leroy Percy, Mississippi Politician, Attorney, and Planter

"Climbing in the mountains in Uganda is not the most challenging climbing by any means," she says. "But for me, it's just the most rewarding kind of climbing because we're having a direct impact on the community."

Regarded as second-class citizens, the women have no ownership rights. The men often abandon the women, leaving them with multiple children to feed. "This opportunity gives these women a sense of confidence and, more than anything, a sense of self-reliance," adds Alison.

Erik Weihenmayer has also made strides to leave the world a better place to live through the No Barriers Foundation. The organization has five focus areas including a virtual event with dozens of adaptive activities, curriculum-based experiences for wounded warriors, a transformative educational program for teens, as well as programs for caregivers and educators.

"Now, more than ever, we need to believe that What's Within Us Is Stronger Than What's in Our Way. Our proven No Barriers framework teaches you step-by-step how to break through your own challenges and live a driven, purposeful life. Despite the barriers—both big and small—that each of us face, we can learn how to push past them, reconnect with our purpose, and unleash the best in ourselves and others," states Erik and his co-founders.

Erik believes that climbing shouldn't be a sport for escape artists trying to avoid the responsibilities of the real world but for taking what we've learned through our expeditions and bringing them back into our lives and into the lives of others. "Having these personal accomplishments with your team is beautiful. But I don't think that's the end game," Erik adds.

"We don't live at the summit or the high point of life. It is a nice goal but what happens when you have to come back down? We live in the valley, and we have to go back and use the encouragement, strength, tools, etc. that we learned on the summit to do something with our life, explains Erik. "The much deeper point is that climbing mountains is selfish and vacant unless you elevate those aroud you with your wisdom. In other words, we need to be conscious of how we use the gifts we earned through the struggle."

The 1000-Year Vision

Most of us lack the ability to think one, five, or ten years ahead. So, the idea of a 1,000-year vision might be mind-blowing and inconceivable. But that's exactly where my friend Marc Butler began when he took over the helm of his parents' company and began adhering to the Toyota Way with his friend and partner, Matt Calkins, by his side.

"We soon discovered that our vision was greater than the sum of our wealth. It was about something bigger. It was very spiritual from the very beginning," says Marc. "What Matt and I do for our employees is transformative for our entire community. It changes families. It changes lives, and it changes the world for the better."

But that discovery didn't come before some difficult tests were handed their way. In 2017, the company JR Butler had figured out how to outmaneuver its competitors and was crushing the market by securing big projects and doing them better, faster, and cheaper than everybody else. But there was a problem. "We never considered that an average campus is somewhere between a half billion and a billion dollars each, and when there was a great pause in the market, I sensed it was going to be a terrible year. But I was going to take care of my people. I was committed to sheltering them. I passed out raises and bonuses as if everything was fine," explains Marc.

Eventually, everything was fine, but not before Matt and Marc stopped trying to shelter their employees and figure things out on their own. They had to lay the cards on the table, engage the community and become the visionaries they were in their very core. That took discipline. "We had the joy in our heart, but we didn't have the discipline in our soul," says Marc. "And the Toyota Way gave us that discipline."

The lean process reshaped the way they did business, and during the year of the great pause, instead of buying into a vision that they were going to lose a million dollars, they decided to make a million. By the end of the year, the company had made

$612,000 — a little short of the mark but much better results than expected.

Then, Marc and Matt also began coaching with executives from Toyota. "What a lot of people don't know about Toyota is they own and operate 3,600 companies in something called the Keiretsu family of companies. And we won the honor of being treated as if we were one of them. We're now seven years into that relationship, and Toyota has signed to be our partner as long as we want their assistance into perpetuity. We've helped Toyota with a business study that's going on to Harvard Business School and all kinds of cool things. We've become very linked in that journey with Toyota the way they teach is tough."

However, that toughness sparked Marc and Matt into transformative thinking, which changed the way they run the business and the manufacturing process of their products. They adopted "Hoshin Kanri (also called Policy Deployment)," which, according to Lean Production, "is a method for ensuring that a company's strategic goals drive progress and action at every level within that company. This method eliminates the waste that comes from inconsistent direction and poor communication."

And improved communication shifts cultures in a positive direction, and the impact can be felt for generations.

My Own 1,000-Year Vision

While Meredith and I have our individual career pursuits, we've also created Denali Venture Philanthropy to support advocacy and education around impact investing. Our organization funds entrepreneurs who are committed to social change. The fund was established to honor and build upon a family legacy of philanthropy by interpreting the legacy in a modern and innovative framework.

Denali Venture Philanthropy was founded on the principle that all people are connected. The universality of the human experience motivates us to improve the lives of others by contributing time, effort, skills, and capital to this mission. Our philosophy is that market forces can, if implemented correctly and fairly, act as a strong mechanism for addressing significant global issues like raising education levels, improving access to quality healthcare, decreasing poverty, and protecting the environment.

Additionally, in 2004, in conjunction with Explorers Club, I established the Seven Summits Awards Program that rewards top students with grants for performing healthcare-related field research. Education is key to bringing more and more people out of poverty and into a higher level of sustenance so that they, too, can continue to pay it forward for years to come.

And my hope is that you, too, will form your own 1,000-year vision and pay your success in life forward for centuries.

Reflection

» How do you define success?

» What are you doing, or could you do to create a stronger community?

» How can you add layers to your experiences?

» What is your 1,000-year vision?

"We pass through the present with our eyes blindfolded... Only later when the cloth is untied can we glance at the past and find out what we have experienced and what meaning it has."

— Milan Kundera, Czech writer

CONCLUSION

IN RETROSPECT

With any expedition, there is a beginning and an end—and then the retrospection of all that's occurred during the journey.

Writing this book has been no different. It's been an expedition, not in the literal sense of climbing a mountain but figuratively.

It began with a calling, a desire to share the leadership and personal growth insights I've garnered over the many miles climbing the Seven Summits and thousands of climbs, expeditions and experiences that followed. Then came the commitment when I began jotting down ideas of what I felt important to discuss in *The Precipice of Life*. Next came pulling together my team—Greg Voisen and Kathy Sparrow—who embraced this vision as if it was their own. That's necessary on the mountain, in business, and in any relationship. No adventure is ever really a solo venture; it takes a team and a collective willingness for everyone to hold the vision and allow it to take on a life of its own. And this one did.

Over time, the vision for this project evolved, and through our collaboration, we invited a multitude of experts to share their unique perspectives on the themes we explored throughout the book. Here are a few ideas we discussed:

- Curiosity—any pursuit begins with a longing to know more—a sense of wonder about what might be possible if we lean into opportunities.

- Commitment—no goal or aim can ever be achieved without the discipline required to stay with an expedition, a project, or a relationship to hang in there even when the going gets tough—and it will.

- Fear—is a normal occurrence whenever we step outside of our comfort zones and broaden our horizons—whether we're climbing a mountain, starting a new business, or taking the next step in a relationship.

- Risk—is necessary. We will never go far in life if we play it safe. That means we have to put our time, energy, hearts, and sometimes our lives on the line.

- Slowing down—as I learned, moving too fast wastes energy and creates disconnection.

- Tuning in—we have so much wisdom available to us if we take the time to listen to the innate wisdom which resides within us.

- Change—as I know all too well from climbing mountains, change is constant and sometimes unpredictable. We never know when the next storm might arise—or even the next opportunity that opens our vistas far beyond our imaginations.

- Resistance—is another name for fear and it keeps us playing a small game—especially when we have new possibilities coming our way—or when we know it's time to leave unhealthy situations.

- Surrender—anytime we're in a situation that requires us to grow, we must let go of our desire to control circumstances, situations, and even outcomes. Our egos die when we surrender, and on the other side is freedom.

- Responsibility—we hold so much power that we often shy away from it. But ultimately, we are responsible for our energy, our time, and even our own happiness.

- And so much more.

The input of the experts quoted within this book added a different dimension to many of the points I wanted to make and always enriched the conversation. This reminds me of those chance meetings on the mountain, where gems of insights and realizations are served over a cup of tea. They're gifts we often didn't expect.

And as this book comes to a close, it's time to look beyond, to another mountain, another precipice, and ask what's next.

I hope you will do the same as you reflect on all that you've taken from this book and consider how you will apply the lessons I've learned on the mountains, in business, and with my relationships to your life.

Of course, not every concept in this book will resonate with you. Take what applies and run with it. And leave room to circle back around to review those concepts that didn't land on the first read—sometimes our resistance is a way to keep us from changing and keep us playing safe.

To facilitate your continued contemplation, you'll find the questions at the end of each chapter on my website www.theprecipiceoflife.com.

May you continue to embrace the precipices of your own life, expand your ability to embrace risk, and come to know more about yourself in the process.

Bo Parfet

"Nobody ever accomplished anything extraordinary by doing what someone else wanted for them."

— David Meltzer

BIBLIOGRAPHY

Adventure Scientists®, Projects, Reports and Publications.
https://www.adventurescientists.org/project-reports-and-
scientific-publications.html.

Avitt, Andrew. "The wellness benefits of the great outdoors."
USDA Forest Service, Office of Communications. March
24, 2021. https://www.fs.usda.gov/features/wellness-
benefits-great-outdoors#:~:text=Being%20outside%20
in%20green%20spaces,quality%20and%20reduce%20
cancer%20risk.%20%20(just%20one%20example)%20
https://www.sharp.com/health-news/5-ways-being-
outdoors-can-make-you-healthier-and-happier.cfm.

Blue Zone. "Friends Nourish the Body and Soul." https://
www.bluezones.com/2012/04/friends-nourish-the-body-
and-soul/.

Branson, Richard. "Working Together to Redefine Dyslexia."
Ask Richard. March 31, 2022. https://www.linkedin.
com/pulse/working-together-redefine-dyslexia-richard-
branson/.

Canfield, Jack. *The Success Principles: How to Get from Where You
Are to Where You Want to Be.* Mariner Books, Boston. 2015.

"Chief Growth Officer Bo Parfet Advises on How to Pick
a Professional Group." Rush PR News. https://www.
rushprnews.com/2021/12/28/chief-growth-officer-bo-
parfet-advises-on-how-to-pick-a-professional-group/.

Clear, James. "My 2016 Integrity Report." James Clear, June 11,
2018. https://jamesclear.com/2016-integrity-report.

Davis, Shirley. "Healing Trauma Through Inner Child Work." CPTSDfoundationorg. https://cptsdfoundation. org/2020/07/20/healing-trauma-through-inner-child-work/.

Dobbs, David. "Restless Genes: The Compulsion to See What Lies Beyond that Far Ridge or That Ocean—or This Planet—Is a Defining Part of Human Identity and Success." *National Geographic*, vol. 223, no. 1, Jan. 2013, pp. 44+. *Gale Health and Wellness*, link.gale.com/apps/doc/A317308132/HWRC?u=nu_main&sid=bookmark-HWRC&xid=a1ad87ec.

"FASTSTATS–Marriage and Divorce." Centers for Disease Control and Prevention. Centers for Disease Control and Prevention, March 25, 2022. https://www.cdc.gov/nchs/fastats/marriage-divorce.htm.

Frederickson, Barbara L. "The Broaden-and-Build Theory of Positive Emotions." *The National Library of Medicine: The Royal Society.* August 17, 2004. https://www.ncbi.nlm.nih.gov/pmc/articles/PMC1693418/.

Glazer, Jessica. "ADHD Can Be a CEO's Secret Superpower. *Huff Post.* September 13, 2016. https://www.huffpost.com/archive/ca/entry/adhd-ceo-career_b_8124154.

Gutman, Ron, "The Hidden Power of Smiling," TedTalk, TED 2011.https://www.ted.com/talks/ron_gutman_the_hidden_power_of_smiling?utm_campaign=tedspread&utm_medium=referral&utm_source=tedcomshare.

Hanson, Rick. "Hardwiring Happiness with Rick Hanson." *Inside Personal Growth.* https://insidepersonalgrowth.com/podcast-497-hardwiring-happiness-with-rick-hanson/.

Hinchcliffe, Emily. "Companies with more women at the top fared better during the pandemic." *The Broadsheet, Fortune.* July 14, 2021 https://fortune.com/2021/07/14/companies-with-more-women-at-the-top-fared-better-during-the-pandemic/.

Hobbs, Jim. "Happiness." http://www.adventurelifereport.com/p/contentment.html.

Holiday, Ryan. *The Obstacle Is the Way: The Timeless Art of Turning Trials Into Triumph.* Portfolio/Penguin. New York, 2014.

Holladay, J. Douglas. *Rethinking Success: Eight Essential Practices for Finding Meaning in Work and Life.* Harper One, New York, 2020.

"Hoshin Kanri." Hoshin Kanri: Policy Deployment Method | Lean Production. https://www.leanproduction.com/hoshin-kanri/#:~:text=Hoshin%20Kanri%20(also%20called%20Policy,inconsistent%20direction%20and%20poor%20communication.

Huffington, Arianna. *Thrive: The Third Metric to Redefining Success and Creating a Life of Well-Being, Wisdom, and Wonder.* Harmony, New York, 2015.

Kashdan, Todd B., and Robert Biswas-Diener. "What Happy people do differently: one of life's sharpest paradoxes is that the key to satisfaction is doing things that feel risky, uncomfortable, and occasionally bad." *Psychology Today*, vol. 46, no. 4, July-Aug. 2013, pp. 50+. *Gale Health and Wellness*, link.gale.com/apps/doc/A335291877/HWRC?u=nu_main&sid=bookmark-HWRC&xid=2ece947b.

Kotler, Steven. "The Art of Impossible-A Peak Performance Primer with Steven Kotler." *Inside Personal Growth*. https://insidepersonalgrowth.com/podcast-839-the-art-of-impossible-a-peak-performance-primer-with-steven-kotler/.

"Laugh More, Lead More" with Naomi Bagdonas and Connor Diemand-Yauman, lecturers at Stanford's Graduate School of Business McKinsey & Company. https://www.mckinsey.com/featured-insights/leadership/laugh-more-lead-better.

Levine, Alison. *On the Edge: Leadership Lessons from Mount Everest and Other Extreme Environments,* Grand Central Publishing, New York, 2014.

Louv, Richard. "The Nature Principle–Overview–Richard Louv." Richard Louv Blog Full Posts Atom 10. *Richard Louv.* https://richardlouv.com/books/nature-principle/.

Magness, Steve. "Changing This 1 Word in Your Thoughts Can Boost Mental Toughness and Resilience, Psychologists Say." CNBC. CNBC, July 1, 2022. https://www.cnbc.com/2022/07/01/how-changing-one-word-in-your-thoughts-can-boost-your-mental-toughness-and-resilience.html?__source=iosappshare%7Ccom.apple.UIKit.activity.Mail.

McKeever, Vicky. "This Country Has Been Named the World's Happiest for the Fifth Year in a Row." CNBC. CNBC, March 18, 2022. https://www.cnbc.com/2022/03/18/finland-named-the-worlds-happiest-for-the-fifth-year-in-a-row.html?&qsearchterm=happiness+report.

Moorefield, Renee. Personal Interview. July 2021. https://www.bewellleadwell.com/.

Moss, Robert. "Sidewalk Oracles with Robert Moss." Inside personal growth. https://insidepersonalgrowth.com/podcast-548-sidewalk-oracles-with-robert-moss/.

Murdock, Jason. "Humans Have More than 6,000 Thoughts per Day, Psychologists Discover." Newsweek. Newsweek, July 15, 2020. https://www.newsweek.com/humans-6000-thoughts-every-day-1517963.

O'Brien, Maryanne. *The Elevated Communicator: How to Master Your Style and Strengthen Your Well-Being at Work.* Simon & Schuster, New York, 2021.

Parfet, Bo with Richard Buskin. *Die Trying: One Man's Quest to Conquer the Seven Summits.* Amacon, New York, 2009.

Parfet, Meredith. "A Hospice Chaplain Shares the Secret to Contentment." Mindful, June 14, 2022. https://www.mindful.org/a-hospice-chaplain-shares-the-secret-to-contentment/.

Piff, Paul K, Pia Dietze, Matthew Feinberg, Daniel M Stancato, and Dacher Keltner. "Awe, the Small Self, and Prosocial Behavior." *Journal of Personality and Social Psychology* 108, no. 6 (2015): 883–899.

Ratey, John, MD. "Podcast 869: ADHD 2.0: New Science and Essential Strategies for Thriving with Distraction–from Childhood through Adulthood with John Ratey," August 3, 2021. *Inside Personal Ggrowth.* https://insidepersonalgrowth.com/?s=ratey.

Rinne, April. *Flux: 8 Superpowers for Thriving in Constant Change.* Berrett-Koehler Publishers, Oakland, CA 2021.

Robinson, Lynn. "Put Your Intuition to Work with
    Lynn Robinson." Inside Personal Growth. https://
    insidepersonalgrowth.com/podcast-648-put-your-
    intuition-to-work-with-lynn-robinson/.

Routen, Ash. "Interview with Reinhold Messner " *Explorersweb*,
    November 16, 2020. https://explorersweb.com/interview-
    with-reinhold-messner/.

Schneider, Gina Simmons, PhD. "Healing Trauma with
    Awe and Wonder." Psychology Today. Sussex
    Publishers. https://www.psychologytoday.com/us/blog/
    frazzlebrain/202111/healing-trauma-awe-and-wonder.

Shiels, Jim. *The Family Board Meeting: You Have 18 Summers
    to Create Lasting Connection with Your Children.* 18
    Summers, 2018.

Shimoff, Marci. *Happy for No Reason: 7 Steps to Being Happy from
    the Inside Out.* Free Press, New York, 2018.

Singer, Michael. The Surrender Experiment: *My Journey into
    Life's Perfection.* Harmony/Rodale, New York, 2015.

Smith, Emily Esfahani. "There's More to Life than Being
    Happy." Emily Esfahani Smith: There's more to life
    than being happy | TED Talk. https://www.ted.com/
    talks/emily_esfahani_smith_there_s_more_to_life_
    than_being_happy?utm_campaign=tedspread&utm_
    medium=referral&utm_source=tedcomshare.

Stevenson, Jane. "What Makes Women CEOs Different?" Korn
    Ferry. Korn Ferry, April 13, 2022. https://www.kornferry.
    com/insights/this-week-in-leadership/women-ceo-insights.

Tseng J, Poppenk J. Brain meta-state transitions demarcate thoughts across task contexts exposing the mental noise of trait neuroticism. Nat Commun. 2020 Jul 13;11(1):3480. doi: 10.1038/s41467-020-17255-9. PMID: 32661242; PMCID: PMC7359033.

Topping, Alexandra "Companies with female leaders outperform those dominated by men, data shows." *The Guardian*, March 6, 2022. https://www.theguardian.com/business/2022/mar/06/companies-with-female-leaders-outperform-those-dominated-by-men-data-shows.

Vayernchuk, Gary. "Here's Where Unhappiness Begins…" YouTube, March 18, 2022. https://youtu.be/xSR7_WM6PM4.

Vivek, Murthy, "Work and the Loneliness Epidemic: Reducing Isolaiton at Work is Good for Business." Harvard Business Review, September 26, 2017. hbr.org/2017/09/work-and-the-loneliness-epidemic.

Voisen, Greg. *Hacking the Gap: A Journey from Intuition to Innovation and Beyond*. Wiseologie Media Group. Encinitas, CA. 2017.

Weber, Alex, *Fail Proof: Become the Unstoppable You,* Post Hill Press, Nashville, 2021.

"We're Here to Redefine Dyslexia." Made By Dyslexia. https://www.madebydyslexia.org/.

Wilson, Hannah. "Want to Boost Your Happiness? Learn Something New." The Happiness Project. The Happiness Project, September 28, 2021. https://the-happiness-project.com/blogs/articles/want-to-boost-your-happiness-learn-something-new.

Winiarski, Pete. *Ignite Your Leadership: Proven Tools for Leaders to Energize Teams, Fuel Momentum and Accelerate Results.* Authors Place Press, Wilmington, NC, 2021.

Wolownick, Dierdre. The Sharp End of Life: A Mother's Story. Mountaineers Books, Seattle, WA. 2019.

Zaki, Jamil. "How to Escape the Cynicism Trap," n.d. https://youtu.be/ABHdTi1If0c.

ACKNOWLEDGMENTS

I want to thank my two boys, Mo and Coco, for being interested in what their dad has to say. They are on their own growth journey, and it's fun to overlap with them. They inspire me to be the best I can be—to be in the moment and put my computer and iPhone down for hours at a time. I love our father-sons' trips. I have a front-row seat to your lives, and I can't wait to see how you make an impact on the world.

To my wife, Meredith, your work as a Hospice Champlin and CEO of a crisis management consulting business is inspiring. You bring lots of positivity and joy to the world. Your role as a mother and wife is something I treasure. Thank you for all you do.

To my parents, Maury and Bill, you both have a zest for life and love of learning that was contagious for me. You were entrepreneurs that found a way to make things work, largely by serving others and being focused on the greater good. Thank you.

To my stepfather, Dick Reed. You were born on a dining room table on a farm in Michigan with no electricity! You become an amazing attorney who helped municipalities get a fair shake. As for being my stepfather, I couldn't have asked for a better one.

To my in-laws Sue, Tim, and John. The way you show up for our family when we needed it most is incredible. I feel so blessed and grateful to have you in my life.

To my boss, Don Wenner, you are an astounding human being. I feel so honored and humbled to work with you at DLP Capital. Thank you for encouraging me—and millions of others to "make an impact."

To Teddy Roosevelt, even though we never met, you made a permanent impact on my life. You showed me that the world is big and fun, and full of opportunities. And that I can be big inside that world. You also showed me that my place shall never be with those cold and timid souls who neither know victory nor defeat.

To Michael Windsor, I am grateful for your artistic genius at creating a cover that captures the spirit of the message of this book.

And of course, my gratitude is immense for my team, Greg Voisen and Kathy Sparrow, who tirelessly dedicated hours upon hours to the interviews, writing, and marketing of *The Precipice of Life: Leadership and Personal Growth Insights from a Mountaineer's Edge.*

ABOUT THE AUTHOR

Bo Parfet
Author and Founder of Denali Venture Philanthropy

A native of Kalamazoo, Michigan, Bo's fire to push boundaries and challenge the status quo have guided him to academic, professional, physical, and personal heights. He began his career in finance as a Research Fellow at the Financial Accounting Standards Board and then transitioned to being an investment banker in corporate finance for J.P. Morgan. During his time on Wall Street, he started an around-the-world journey to climb the Seven Summits, the highest mountain on every continent, which he completed with Mount Everest in 2007.

Having tackled some of the world's highest peaks, Bo is currently the Managing Principal responsible for growth at DLP

Capital, an innovative real estate solutions provider dedicated to tackling broad social issues and leading with courage.

Bo is an active philanthropist and innovator in the area of social entrepreneurship. In 2004, in conjunction with The Explorers Club, Bo established the Seven Summits Awards Program that rewards top students with grants to perform healthcare-related field research. In 2013, Bo founded Denali Venture Philanthropy to formally fuse his love of business with his desire to support positive change in the world.

Bo holds a master's degree in Economics from the University of Michigan, an MBA from the Kellogg School of Management at Chicago's Northwestern University, and a BS in Economics from Colorado State University. He is the author of *Die Trying: One Man's Quest to Conquer the Seven Summits* and *They Lived to Tell the Tale: True Stories of Modern Adventure from the Legendary Explorers Club.*

For more about Bo and his books, visit
www.boparfet.com and
www.theprecipiceoflife.com/

To contact Bo for speaking engagements, please
email him at: bo@theprecipiceoflife.com

**For photos of some of his expeditions, see
www.theprecipiceoflife.com/gallery**

MEET MY TEAM

Literary Midwife Kathy Sparrow

Literary Midwife Kathy Sparrow is an award-winning author, ghostwriter, and publishing consultant who has been mentoring aspiring writers of non-fiction, fiction, and poetry for over two decades. Many have penned bestselling books because of her book coaching services. Known as a "behind-the-scenes secret weapon" to thought leaders, Kathy specializes in the areas of self-development, leadership, and memoir.

Kathy is the co-author and project lead of *Ignite Your Leadership: Proven Tools for Leaders to Energize Teams, Fuel Momentum, and Accelerate Results.* Her novel, *The Whispered Teachings of Grandmother Trout,* is touted as the feminine version of A *River Runs Through It.* She is co-author of the children's books, *Stanky & Cece: Break the Rules (2022)* and *Stanky & Cece: Out of Control* (2023). She is completing *It's All in the Cast: A Fly Fisher's Guide to Presence, Power & Performance* (2023). She has ghostwritten books and blogs on the topics of banking, personal growth and development, memoir, and leadership

Throughout her career, she has worked with IDG Press (the former *For Dummies* publisher), Master's Press, Wish Publishing, ARE Press, and others. Her work as a journalist has also appeared in *Saltwater Fly Fishing, Indianapolis Woman, Indiana Business Magazine, E magazine, Hudson Valley Magazine,* and many more. A university professor, she has taught writing in first-year writing programs, sophomore literature, theatre, and marketing for authors.

Kathy has studied transformational methodologies with Jack Canfield founder of *Chicken Soup for the Soul* and author of *The Success Principles*, Dr. Deb Sandella of The RIM® Institute, Laurie Seymour of The Baca Institute, and Renee Moorefield of Wisdom Works. She is a Certified Canfield Trainer in The Success Principles and Canfield Methodologies, Certified Be Well Lead Well Pulse® Guide, and Master RIM® facilitator. Kathy relies on the science of success tools to assist her clients in overcoming obstacles and mindset limitations, as well as identify how to create a life filled with vitality and well-being. She holds a master's degree in English with a concentration in literature and cultural studies.

Kathy enjoys yoga, hiking, fly fishing, and adventures with her partner and family. She spends her time in LA and San Diego, and you can also find her in Colorado, Mexico, Oregon—or wherever her travels take her. Her websites are: www.kathysparrow.com and www.awritablelife.com

Greg Voisen, Founder of Inside Personal Growth

Greg Voisen is a thought leader in the personal growth and human potential movement. He is a speaker, author, entrepreneur, and philanthropist.

Founder of *Inside Personal Growth*, a popular podcast where Greg has interviewed over 970 authors on the topics of personal growth, business, wellness, and spirituality.

He is the co-author of *Wisdom, Wellness and Redefining Work* and the author of *Hacking the Gap: From Intuition to Innovation and Beyond*. Both books are focused on improving the journey toward higher human potential by way of experience and applying new learned skills to achieve optimal performance.

Greg is the executive director of his non-profit called *Compassionate Communications Foundation* where his mission is to assist the homeless by helping them to start a journey of transitioning from living on the streets to moving into sustainable housing.

He has bachelor's degree from San Diego State University in Business Management and a master's in Spiritual Psychology from University of Santa Monica.

To learn more about Greg you can visit his websites:

www.eluminate.net

www.insidepersonalgrowth.com

www.gregvoisen.com

www.hackingthegap.com

www.compassionate communications.org

Printed in the USA
CPSIA information can be obtained
at www.ICGtesting.com
LVHW070723261023
761974LV00029B/384/J